My Service Dog's Place

By: Kelly Kowall
Gold Star Mother of SPC Corey Kowall

Copyright © 2023 Kelly Kowall. All rights reserved. No part of this publication may be reproduced, distributed, or transmitted in any form or by any means, including photocopying, recording, or other electronic or mechanical methods, without the prior written permission of the author, except in the case of brief quotations embodied in critical reviews and specific other noncommercial uses permitted by copyright law. For permission requests, write to the author, addressed: Attention: Kelly Kowall, at kelly.mwp@gmail.com

Contents

Dedication	5
Acknowledgment	6
Prelude	7
1 "The Nightmare"	11
2 "The Notice"	26
3 "Goodbyes & Hellos'	31
4 "Rocky"	37
5 "Insanity?"	41
6 "Homecoming"	47
7 "Youth"	53
8 "At Least We Are Friends"	58
9 "Emails Home"	62
10 "Coming Home"	72
11 "COP Zerok"	84
12 "First Impressions"	96
13 "XinHua"	107
14 "The Funeral"	113

15 "War Is Hell	117
16 "The Calls"	125
17 "Six"	132
18 "Thanksgiving Day Wishes"	142
19 "My Service Dog's Place"	155
20 "Christmas Together"	163
21 "New Beginnings"	172
22 "It's In The Stars"	182
Epilogue	191
Resource Books	197
About MWP and its Programs	199

Dedication

To my parents who never stopped believing in me. To my brother who encouraged me. To my son who inspired me from heaven. To my bond family and friends who supported me and cheered me on when I struggled. And to those who read this, may you find the love, courage, joy, and inspiration contained within these pages.

Acknowledgements

While this story is fictional it has been based on factual events and circumstances.

For the privacy of some whom I interviewed for this book, I will only be sharing first names in this acknowledgment except for R. Glenn Kelly who helped me get this book out of my head and onto paper.

To the Veterans John, Jon, Robby and Bill, who were willing to share their stories with me during their time in theater and/or their time spent in Civil Air Patrol and JROTC, I cannot thank you enough for being so open and candid.

Also, thank you to Gold Star Parents, Shannon and Mitch for allowing me to share a part of their painful story and loss.

And last, but not least, thank you to all my family, friends and acquaintances who were willing to read and re-read my book, helping me to edit, and encourage me to write the next chapter.

PRELUDE "Letter Home - RIP"
January 19, 1973

Dear Dad,

Yesterday was probably the worst day I have ever lived in my entire, short life. Once again, we were in contact with Charlie, and once again, we suffered losses. The losses we had yesterday, though, really hit home hard as my best friend in this shit hole was killed. Bennie was the same age as me, dad. Only 19 years old. I feel that if I had moved a little quicker, just a half-a-second sooner, maybe he would still be alive.

Strange how short a time a half-second is… the difference between life and death. Just this morning, we had been talking about how we were only two months different in age and how we had both left a girl back home. You know, I can still feel his presence as I write this letter. I just hope that I can survive and leave all of this far behind me, but I'm really afraid I will never be the same. Why him and not me? Who decides that?

At 1400 today, the memorial service took place. The most difficult part was when our First Sergeant called the final roll. He called the names of each member of our squad, and each answered in turn. Then Bennie's name was called once, no response. Twice, no response. The third time his name was called, even though I knew he was dead, I was praying so hard that I would hear him answer. I wanted to hear him so bad, and it just killed me when there was no response again. Then "Taps" began to play, accompanied by a "21-gun salute." We then filed by his helmet atop his rifle, dog tags hanging from it, all of this behind his boots, and a picture of him. Each of us, individually, turned to his equipment and rendered a final salute. We had no time to linger as we were expected to get back into formation. The Chaplin then said a few words, and we were dismissed. It's like we are expected to put it behind us just like that.

I know this is probably harder for you to read than it was for me to write. If there is a place called HELL, this surely must be it. I keep asking myself if there is a God. I am not sure anymore because if there was a God, why the hell did he allow young men with so much to live for die in this god-forsaken place? I just hope that his death and the deaths of all the others are not in vain.

I look forward to the day when I get to come home. If I play my cards right, I should be able to come home in the next few months. The reason I say this is because, by March, I will have more than enough time in-country.

I hope that tomorrow is quiet. We will be going into base camp soon for our three-day stand down. I will try and write you a longer letter at that time.

Please don't worry too much about me. I promise to take care of myself, and I look forward to the day I will be with you and Mom again.

Love,
Tom

P.S. Do you remember the stray dog that I was telling you about in the last letter? Bennie and I had named him Rocky. I am really hoping I can somehow bring Rocky home with me. I know you and Mom would love him. He is so smart. He seems to somehow know that Bennie is gone. Strange how dogs can be so intuitive.

Chapter 1 "The Nightmare"
November 2, 2012

Army Private Thomas "Tom" Johnson, a lean and muscular man with a sturdy physique, and Private Benjamin "Bennie" Filmore find their way over to a rickety thatch hut that had recently been liberated from the Vietcong.

Breathing heavily, as they had just escaped a clever ambush, they move inside to join two marines just sitting about taking a break in this recently recovered oasis in the jungle. They sit and exchange small talk for a bit when Tom carelessly picks up a pebble, tosses it into the air, and opens his hand to catch it as he mutters, "Man, Bennie, it was some kind of hell down there on that ridge. They had us, you know? If it weren't for them choppers showing up, we'd be gone, my friend."

"Nah, Tom…no way. I'm trying my best not to die out here in these boondocks. So I damn sure ain't letting nothing happen to you either." Slapping Tom on his back, Bennie ensures, "You're my brother. And that, I tell you, means I've got your back."

"Yeah… I don't know, Bennie. I've known all my life I'd be here, you know. Creepy, isn't it? I've always felt it. And if this is where I'm supposed to be when I die, at least I'm going out fighting, right?"

"You're crazy, man! You ain't going nowhere. You might go out fighting Tom, but not here." Bennie says. "I won't let that happen. No, sir, not on my watch."

Just at that moment, something small and oddly round silently rolls inside the hut, and someone in the group shouts, "Grenade!"

Tom instinctively moves toward the grenade, thinking he has time to grab it and throw it back outside before it explodes.

Just as his outreached fingertips almost touch the round, metal orb, he's unexpectedly jerked back. Bennie had grabbed him by the flack jacket and, being a strong and sizable young fellow, literally turned Tom around and quickly moved him toward the exit of the hut, pushing him out the door.

As Tom's body clears the makeshift door frame, the grenade explodes, and the concussion wave lifts and carries both men some ten feet outside the structure. For the next few moments, all is still and eerily quiet as the last parts of splintered trees and tropical foliage seem to rain back down to earth. The air is filled with enough dust that he can't see what lies a foot ahead. He could smell metal, gunpowder, and burning flesh in the atmosphere.

Bennie is lying belly down with his arms splayed wide. He is unable to feel his body, but he can see Tom just a few feet to his left. He tries to get up but can't. It feels as if his entire body has gone numb. Or was he paralyzed? Either way, he couldn't reach the friend he was watching, who seemed to be lying on the ground unconscious. What he then observes is Tom suddenly bolting up into a sitting position. His face looks almost normal, though. There are burn marks, and his helmet hangs back over his head, caught only by the chin strap, but Tom has a casual expression on his face as he scans the area, as if trying to fathom what has actually happened.

When Tom's gaze turns toward him, Bennie sees his eyes widen, but Tom's calm expression never changes. Even as he sees Tom get up and walk over with a slight limp towards him, Tom seems so calm.

Bennie tried to move again but couldn't. He tries to say Tom's name, but oddly, nothing comes out of his mouth. He tries to scream, but he feels a suffocating silence. When Tom gets near Bennie, he kneels by his side and leans over his face, trying to assess his injuries. Bennie had never seen Tom look so scared.

Bennie tries to speak again. However, by then, he has understood perhaps something isn't right with him; he is hurt. How bad? He didn't know. Tom reaches out his left hand and touches Bennie's cheek as if to check his temperature, and with the other hand, he checks his wrist to understand if his condition is stable. Suddenly Bennie's body begins to twitch convulsively; Tom watches as Bennie's eyes slowly go listless.

Tom then leans over to his friend to check his eyes. Bennie sees Tom's worried expression on his face as he begins to lose sight of Tom. His surroundings begin to fade to black, and within a moment, everything vanishes.

Moving quickly, Tom rolls the bloody body of his friend over and onto his own lap, realizing that his dear friend's soul has certainly just left the body. He was gone.

Tom looks around for a moment and then turns his gaze to the hut. Gently laying his friend's body on the bare ground, he quickly moves over to where the door used to be of what was left of the thatched roof structure and peers inside. It is instantly apparent that everyone inside is dead. Just as Tom drops his head in despair, however, he hears the sound of incoming enemy troops – the unmistakable rattle and whine of Vietnamese troop carriers. They were just over the next ridge. He had to find a weapon in all this carnage. He would set himself up somewhere around the thatched hut and defend the remains of his comrades. These little Charlie bastards would not get the privilege of seeing what they had done. They didn't even leave him a chance to mourn his friend.

Limping upside the hill, he finds what seems to be a functional fifty-caliber machine gun and crouches down behind a large tree. He catches a glimpse of something just to his right. Turning, he is shocked to see his son Joseph (Joey) standing there with one hand on the top of his head and another holding a bicycle wheel.

"Joey! Joey? Is that you, boy?" He is bewildered seeing his son there. "What the hell are you doing here?"

"The wheel, Dad." Joey says, "You gotta fix this wheel and help me get out of here."

Joey then abruptly turns and, without another word, walks quickly behind the grenade-torn thatched hut and out of his dad's sight. Stunned, Tom knows he has to go after his son. Bolting from his defensive position, Tom runs around the corner of the hut, but instead of finding his son, he finds a single Jeep with the left rear up on a jack and two tires lying flat on the ground. Still searching for his son, Tom walks past the Jeep in the only direction his son could have gone. That takes him to a steep incline down the ridge, where monsoon rains and the ravages of war had eroded almost every bit of vegetation. If his son truly had been there and gone over this ridge, Tom would certainly have seen him now. Yet he is nowhere to be seen. He blinks his eyes, thinking it has all been a mirage or something.

Tom hears the sounds of the enemy troops approaching again. Quickly he sprints back towards the Jeep. He assumes that the vehicle had been in the mid-flat repair when the Marines working on it had taken a break to go inside the hut and lounge for a bit. Regardless, Tom runs to the tires and uses his foot to kick each one, finding the intended spare. Tossing the sling of the fifty-caliber machine gun over his shoulder, he literally throws the tire onto the axle hub and, as fast as he could, spins three of the ten required lugs on the bolts, hand tightening them as much as his bleeding fingers would allow. With all the speed he could muster, he lowers the jack, throws it aside, jumps behind the wheel of the Jeep, and fires her up. Tom quickly turns the Jeep around and drives to where Bennie's body lies on the ground. Throwing it into a park, Tom jumps out, swoops Bennie up in his arms, and then places him in the back of the Jeep. He wasn't going to leave his friend behind. He couldn't. Jumping back into the Jeep, he shifts into first gear. Just as Tom stomps on the Jeep's gas pedal, four Vietnamese troop carriers come crashing through the edge of the jungle and begin circling the Jeep, the enraged enemy screaming loudly and waving the rifles in the air. Tom was caught. There was no way out of this now…

Tom suddenly bolts awake in his bed, covered in sweat. Another night terror. Although he had been having them ever since he had gotten back from Vietnam, this one was different. This was the first time his son Joey had ever been in one of his nightmares. He blamed himself for allowing him to join the army. He should've put his foot down and said no. He knew all too well that some of them didn't come home. Tom crawls out of bed and makes his way into the kitchen, where he grabs a glass and pours himself a stiff drink. He looks at the clock. 5:10 am.

"The same time," he mumbles to himself. The same time his life was shattered forever when his son Joey was killed at the COP (Combat Outpost) in Afghanistan.

Sitting alone at his kitchen table with a stiff drink in his hand, Tom contemplates selling the place, buying an RV, and hitting the road after he retires in just a few more years. After all, he really had nothing holding him to this one-horse town anymore. Ever since he had received the knock on the door 15 days ago, informing him that his son had been killed in Afghanistan, his life had gone from bad to worse. Yes, there were a few veterans that he got together with once in a while to play some poker, smoke cigars, and drink. And then there was his lady friend, Annie, who worked at the dog pound in the next town over, but he didn't see that relationship going anywhere. He had closed his heart off a long time ago. It was easier that way. Yeah, it might mean that he would be all by himself most of the time, but at least it wouldn't hurt when they disappeared from his life.

He had let himself go like the house he lived in. The fence needed mending, the house needed a good scrubbing, the outside needed to be painted, and the yard and landscaping were overgrown and needed to be trimmed, but he didn't care.

Damn, those dreams... each time, a different glimpse of the place that he never wanted to revisit. However, each one ended on the same note, the feeling of being caught.... by what he did not know. He remembers, as a soldier, taking the oath to give his life if necessary. Death wasn't something he was scared of. It was something else – perhaps losing his soul on the battlefield, he guessed. For the last few weeks, what little sleep he had been able to get was now rarely becoming his companion. The moment the sun sets and it gets dark, some unwanted memories grab ahold of his mind. He didn't know what to call them, hallucination, illusion, a disturbing memory, perhaps. But it transports him back to the place he keeps trying to run away from.

Now nursing his fourth straight whiskey before 8:30 am, he feels a strong wave of grief washing over him. He'd been able to push it back before, but this time it was very strong. Trying to hold it back, he fails and literally screams aloud as he lets it out. Suddenly he hears his son's voice in his mind...clear...crisp….and loud! "Way ta go, Dad...bring it out...bring it out and into the light."

It's as clear as if he heard it through his ears, but this was in his mind. He shakes his head in disbelief, thinking it is whisky-induced, and blows it off. He swallows hard from what's left in his glass before making another full pour. As he does, however, another grief wave strikes and brings with it the images of his son intermixed in his mind with the images of his lost battle buddy in Nam...angered he throws the glass at the wall, and it shatters, falling to the floor with what was left of the ice and booze. A single tear runs down his face.

"Good, Dad...now you're getting it….now you're bringing out," he hears in his head, loud and clear again. He abruptly stands this time, pushing the kitchen chair almost halfway across the room with the flexing back of his legs. He scans the room with quick, jerking motions and, seeing nothing, shoots across the floor, through the door, and into the living room. Seeing no one there, he turns and slowly walks back into the kitchen, where he grabs another tumbler, pours himself another full glass of whiskey, and puts it to his lips. Just as he's about to tip it up to take it all down in one gulp, he becomes oddly enveloped in a warmth...a warmth that feels as if every inch of his body is being gently squeezed by some unseen force.

It might be unseen, but somehow he realizes what it is...his son is there with him. Not in front of him but all around him. He feels him inside and outside his body. The feeling and the simple acknowledgment that his son was there becomes overwhelming, and he drops slowly to his knees, bows his head, and his shoulders begin to shake.

Through growing sobs, he raises his head and says the only words that come to his mind… "I miss you, son. God, how I miss you…."

"I know, Dad," his son replies, as the words seem to vibrate through every cell in his body. "I miss being next to you while we're working on the old pickup truck out in the barn. I miss going fishing with you and talking about life while waiting for the fish to bite. I just miss being able to just stand beside you, Dad. And your hugs… I miss your hugs. But I'm here, Dad… I've always been here, and I always will be."

"Oh God, son…I must be losing my mind. Whaddya mean you've always been here? This can't be real."

Suddenly anger boils in his tricky mind. Yeah, surely it's his fickle mind playing tricks on him. There's no other explanation. He's either going nuts...or more nuts than he was before, or the booze is screwing with his noggin. With that, he angrily picks up the half-empty bottle of whiskey and hurls it across the room, where it shatters in a fluid and glass explosion against the tile behind the sink. With that, another scream of anger and the warmth dissipates from around his body. All is quiet.

"Buddy?" Nothing. "Son?" Stillness in the air.

Chapter 2 "The Notice"
August 1, 1971

Driving back home from the store, Tom stops at the mailbox near the beginning of the dirt lane that leads up to the family homestead. He had seen the mail truck pass him on the road, so he knew the mailman had delivered the mail. Hopping out of the car, he walks over to the box, opens the lid, and reaches inside to retrieve the contents. Casually sorting through the envelopes as he walks back to the car, he stops suddenly and freezes. His eyes are fixed on the return address. It is from the Selective Service System and addressed to him. He knows instinctively what the letter is because some of his friends have already been drafted. Even though he knows what the piece of paper inside this envelope says, he is too unnerved to open it. He does not want to. Not yet, anyway.

He jumps back into the car, throws the mail onto the passenger seat, and drives up the lane to the house. He is still shaken as he gathers up the letters, walks up the sidewalk, and steps through the front door. No one is in the kitchen when he enters. He slumps down into a chair and throws the mail on the table in front of him.

I want to sit here for a while, with the decision of my future in my hand, he thinks as he picks up the letter addressed to him. Like in limbo, his life, as it is, balances the reality of the moment and what the future will hold.

The suspense of what is about to come is overwhelming. He is frightened to discover his fate, but he knows he can't keep the letter sealed forever. So, with a beating heart, he tears open the envelope and unearths the beige piece of paper inside. *This can't be possible,* he thinks. He can feel the blood drain from his head, and the room begins to spin. The kitchen clock is ticking somewhere in the room, and its sound is as loud as a hammer striking a metal anvil.

He stares at the paper in front of him for a moment. Then he draws it closer to his face to get a better look. Had he seen things correctly? Surely not. This has to be a terrible mistake. He reads it again. "You are hereby ordered for induction into the Armed Forces of the United States and to report..."

He gasps, and the faded yellow piece of paper that had become damp and curled from his grip falls from his hand. He groans. A groan that would have turned into a shriek of shock if he was to let it out. He picks up the paper from the floor as his eyes begin re-reading the whole letter. He scans it all in one go, not realizing he is holding his breath as he reads. It was all true. No matter how much he tries to deny it. No matter how much his eyes did not want to believe it. Beginning to tremble, he grips the edge of the kitchen table. Another fearful cry starts to rise in his chest, but this one erupts as a strangled gasp as he struggles to contain it within. He couldn't... no, he wouldn't let his emotions get the best of him.

So as his mind tries to settle on it, like a deer caught in the headlights, he realizes that his life is about to change forever.

In the following days, his life was filled with uncertainties and uneasiness. He was consumed with the thought that he would soon be going away. He was wholly immersed in his life at home, working on the farm, so swapping it for this new life away from his family was nothing short of life-altering. Strangely, he is not quite sure how all of this has happened. He didn't know who he could blame, unaware of who had a hand in this life-changing decision.

Was this karma? Was this fate? He wasn't sure. But he guesses now it didn't really matter. He hears all kinds of things from his family. They are trying to help him cope. Like the threads that become imperceptible in a piece of cloth, so did individual voices trying to give him any advice.

He is sure that his family was faking their support. After all, there was no "bright side." Their advice sounded forced, the enthusiasm influenced. They were trying too hard to make it seem natural, but it was apparent they were just as sad and scared as he was...if not more.

Chapter 3 "Goodbyes & Hellos"
September 4, 1971 – March 5, 1972

The next few weeks go by in a blur. He doesn't remember when he packed his bags or what was said when he said goodbye to his family. The sensation of setting off from home seems so final. He feels the tightness in his chest and throat as he holds back the tears. He is determined not to let them see him cry. It is almost like an out-of-body experience because the next thing he knows, he is on a bus bound for Fort Wayne in Michigan. He guessed this is why he's always had ambivalent feelings about leaving home since.

He decides to dress for the occasion by arriving in his favorite bell-bottom jeans and a black t-shirt with multi-color tie-dyed wording of Love at the top, the word Peace at the bottom, and a huge peace sign in the middle. It is his way of silently protesting against the war and being forced to serve in the military.

He sits next to the window and just watches the landscape go by for the next few hours. As the bus starts to slow down at the gate, he can see that the Fort is situated on the Detroit River, and the original 1848 limestone barracks are still standing.

Upon arrival, they are all quickly ordered off the bus and taken to an area where they are sworn in and given their shots. Then they are ordered to board another bus to take them to Ft. Knox for Basic Training.

He finds a seat by the window once again, waiting on the rest of the guys who are boarding to find their seats, when this guy wearing the exact t-shirt says, "I see you wanted to make a statement too!"

The voice grabs his attention, and for the first time, he looks away from the window towards the guy wearing the exact same shirt as him.

"Great t-shirt! My name is Benjamin. Benjamin Filmore, but everyone calls me Bennie. Do you mind if I sit next to you?" He asks as he extends his hand for a handshake.

"It's fine by me," he replies as they shake hands. "My name is Tom. So, where are you from?"

Bennie shares his life details with Tom – where he was from, where he lived, what his family was like, and about the girl he left back home.

Tom soon realizes the two of them have a lot in common, from their taste in shirts to their home lives. They both chuckle at the fact that they know they will be bringing on some sort of punishment by those in charge when they arrive at the Fort due to their choice of attire, but they hadn't cared.

As they suspected, they both got smoked over their attire. Bennie, just like him, had been quickly ordered off the bus upon arrival at the base and forced to drop and give them 20. Tom thinks his arms will give out before he ekes out those 20 pushups, but he manages to complete them because he sure isn't going to give them the satisfaction of seeing him fail. Of course, Bennie has no problems whipping out 20 as he had just completed his varsity year on the high school football team and loved working out in the gym. In fact, they made Bennie do 50 more, stating that they would wipe the smile off his face. But the two begin to realize that the training they will be getting in basic isn't going to be like any training they had received in the high school gym.

Their first day at basic is destined to make a very distinct impression on them –something that will stay with them for a long time. It is like reality hitting them in the face.

Even though basic training was brutal and pushed them to their limits, at least Bennie and Tom had been assigned to the same squad, so the eight weeks at Ft.

Knox seem to fly by. Luckily, they both get chosen to attend six weeks at Fort Polk for AIT (Advanced Individual Training), which is similar to a trade school, and they learn the technical skills needed for their specific Army MOS (Military Occupational Specialties). Then they are both chosen to be sent back to Ft. Knox for two weeks of APC (Armored Personnel Carrier) training. There they learn how to drive specific armored personnel vehicles designed to transport personnel and equipment into combat zones.

It is crazy that upon completing their training, both Bennie and Tom are handed a commercial plane ticket to Oakland, CA, so that they can report to the Oakland Army Base. From there, they are taken to San Francisco International Airport, where they board a Tiger Airlines plane, which flies them to Alaska, where it refuels. The reality is starting to sink in that they are now heading to a combat zone. The plane then flies to Japan, where it refuels once more before dropping them off in Vietnam.

The heat is stifling and hits Tom like a ton of bricks as he deplanes. A feeling of strangeness oppresses him as he begins to realize the grimness of the situation that lies ahead of him here in this jungle. He has already started counting the days until he will be able to leave this hell hole and go home.

Chapter 4 "Rocky"
February 23, 1973

Dear Dad,

I don't know if I can go on after what happened today. I was out on patrol with Jake, and all of a sudden, Rocky came barreling out of the jungle, running right past me and into a small clearing. He was barking and growling like a dog on a mission. The commotion stopped us in our tracks. I was about to yell at him when suddenly, a shot rang out. I heard Rocky yelp and saw him flip over in the air, landing on his side. I wanted to rush over to him, but Jake was holding me back.

We ducked down and watched as a few VCs came out from the dense foliage and made their way over to where Rocky lay. One started kicking him along his back, and another took the end of his rifle and jabbed it in his chest. Rocky lay there thrashing as if trying to get up, and I could hear him whimpering in pain. After what seemed like an eternity, the third one raised his rifle and shot him in the head. All three started laughing and slapping each other on the back as if they had done something good. Then they turned around and walked back into the jungle as if nothing had happened.

It was excruciating watching them torture Rocky and not being able to stop it without putting Jake in jeopardy. If I had been by myself, I would have started shooting. They would have got me for sure, but not without me taking at least one of them out first for killing Rocky.

I still can't believe it, Dad. I don't know how Rocky got out of camp. Ever since Bennie was killed, Rocky was constantly by my side except when I had to leave and go out on patrol. He didn't like me to leave, but he would always stay in camp and wait until I returned. But not today. It makes me wonder, did he somehow know that Jake and I would have been ambushed? Is that why he escaped camp so that he could save Jake and me?

Jake wanted to get back to camp right away, but I talked him into staying long enough for Charlie to leave so that I could retrieve Rocky's body. I was able to bury him back at camp, and the guys all helped me lay him to rest. I still can't believe he is gone.

I feel so broken, Dad. I just don't know how I am ever going to get over this. First, Benny, and now Rocky. Why them and not me? It should have been me. I wish it had been me. I keep going over and over it in my head. I keep hearing that one shot that rang out, putting a bullet into Rocky's head. I told you before that this place is hell. It must be because I sure can't think of anything worse.

It is so hard. To just keep stuffing it and trudging on. To have to keep going like nothing has happened. How do you survive this?

I should be leaving to come stateside in two weeks. I will let you know when I can get leave to come home. I miss you.

Love,
Tom

P.S. If you talk to Mom, please tell her that I love her and miss her.

Chapter 5 "Insanity?"
November 2, 2012

The phone rings. Tom can see by the caller ID that it is Annie. He really likes her, but he doesn't see any future for them. After all, she loves dogs, and he doesn't ever want a dog in his life again. He has never gotten over the loss of Rocky, and he doesn't want to go through the heartache of getting so attached to an animal ever again. It just hurts too much when they are gone from your life. He guesses that it is the same reason he doesn't want to get too involved with people too. It is just easier being alone and not getting into any strong bond or relationship. Then you are not devastated when they leave you. He isn't sure he wants to talk with anyone right now, but he answers the phone anyway, "Hi Annie, what's up?"

"Hey, Tom. I just wanted to call and see how you were doing. Is there anything I can do for you?" Annie can tell he has been drinking and is concerned. After all,

Tom had just buried his son three days ago, and she wanted to be there for him.

"I don't know," Tom replies, "I am still trying to comprehend it all. And I think I am starting to go insane."

"What do you mean?" Annie asks inquisitively.

"I know this is going to sound crazy, but I think my son is trying to contact me. I swear I heard his voice this morning and felt his presence. And yes, I have been drinking... but I swear it is true. I don't know how to really describe it, but I have been feeling it for a while now. And then this morning was just insane."

"I believe you, Tom. I don't think you are going crazy," Annie says reassuringly. "In fact, one of my girlfriends had a son who was killed on a combat mission in Afghanistan, and she swears she was contacted by him almost immediately. She told me that at first, she was afraid to say anything because she didn't want to be put in a straitjacket and hauled off to the funny farm. But after a while, she started sharing with me, and a few others, about how he had been contacting her."

"Really?" Tom questions, his curiosity now piqued. "In what way was she contacted?"

"Well, she said that at first, he seemed to be trying to contact her through billboards. Then, in dreams. Later on, she said she swore she heard his voice telling her that things would be ok and that he loved her. She also said that one night she even got a text message from him. Now that one really freaked her out!"

"Hmmmm. Maybe I'm not going cuckoo after all." Tom softly replies. "Annie, I don't know if I am going to survive this. I can't seem to function. My head is in a fog. I just seem to be going through the motions. Thank God my body knows how to breathe because I am not sure I would have the strength nor the presence of mind to breathe if my body needed to be told to do so." Tom pauses, and although he stops talking, Annie knows not to say anything, to just let it hang there until he is ready to start talking again. After a bit, Tom continues, "I am having the dreams again. But this time, they are different. Now Joey is starting to come into them."

"How so?" asks Annie.

"It's weird. They are the same nightmares I often have of my time in Nam, but then suddenly, he appears as a child at a very odd time in the dream. It's so confusing."

It is rare that Tom talks about his time in Vietnam with her, but she is glad that he feels comfortable enough in their relationship to share his pain on rare occasions. She really likes Tom and enjoys spending time with him, but she isn't sure that their relationship will ever develop beyond dating. It concerns her that he drinks to medicate himself. That he is always on guard and can't relax in a crowd, which limits where they can go when out and about. And sometimes, he even scares her a bit when he wakes up from a night terror since it takes him a moment to realize it is her next to him in bed and not the enemy.

"Annie, I don't like where I am right now. I thought it couldn't get any worse. I mean, with all I had to see and do while in Nam, I couldn't imagine anything worse. I can still remember looking through the site of my gun and seeing a VC firing his weapon at us. I put him in my crosshairs and took my shot. All I know is that the next thing I saw was a red mist shoot up in the air where his head used to be, and I saw his body drop. Does the Taliban soldier, who killed my son, have this burned into his memory the way all those I killed are burned in mine?"
"When I first got to Nam, I was hyped up like the rest of my squad. I had been told that Charlie was evil. That they were the enemy. But after being over there for a

while, after being face to face and up close and personal for a bit, I began to realize that they were human, just like me. It became harder and harder to separate that in my head. Then having to reconcile all of that with the fact that I was the one killing them. I had to start stuffing it just to get through my time over there. And then when Bennie was killed... and then Rocky..." Tom begins to sob.

"I can't even begin to imagine Tom," says Annie in a hushed tone. "I'm going to come over. Is that ok?"

"Yes, it's ok," she hears Tom choke out before she hears the click of him hanging up.

Annie then jumps out of her chair, grabs her keys and purse, and sprints to her car. In a flash, she is on her way to Tom's place.

Chapter 6 "Homecoming"
March 2, 1973 – February 1, 1989

Tom is grateful to be back home as his plane ride from Nam comes to an end. So much so that he feels the urge to kiss the tarmac once he gets off the plane, but he doesn't. The sky is a bright shade of blue, and fluffy white clouds drift overhead. He feels a sense of relief and gratitude to be back in the United States, but the emotions he expects to feel are elusive. He had imagined feeling joyful and free, but his experiences in the war still weighed heavily on him. In his mind, he thought he would be able to leave it all behind him. To close that chapter in his life like you would close a door behind you and not look back. But it isn't like that at all. While he is happy to be home, he doesn't feel joyful. Will he ever feel joy again? Will he be able to find true happiness? He is doubting it now. He wants it, but after having to do things that go against his religious and moral upbringing, such as "thou shall not kill," he isn't so sure anymore. Even though it had been "kill or be killed" and not something, he freely chose to do, having to do so had changed him forever. And, just because he is back in the US, he still has at least two more years before he gets out of the Army. Talk is that the war is winding down, but if it doesn't, he will be sent back for another tour, and he isn't sure he will survive it.

It angers him when someone calls him a "baby killer" or spits on him. What gives them the right to judge him or anyone else who serves? They had no clue as to who he was. After all, those who are drafted don't have a choice unless they are willing to take the cowards' way out and flee to Canada. Are these people so stupid as not to understand that they had the freedom of speech and the right to protest due to those who were willing to go and fight for these rights? Do they not understand that the fight in Vietnam was to defend the sovereign nation of South Vietnam to keep them free from Communism? Would these same fools not want another nation to come and defend the United States if we are threatened? And he didn't care what anyone said; politics was involved, and that is a whole other issue.

Why not spit on the politicians? Why not call them "killers" or promoters of child labor. And these protesters of the war, weren't they supposed to be promoting peace and love?? He didn't see or feel anything peaceful or loving, only hateful words and actions. What hypocrites!

Although his time in the Army comes to an end, he just can't seem to get back to being the happy-go-lucky Tom that he was prior to going to Nam.

He struggles with relationships, so he surprises himself when he meets a young lady named Jackie right after his 31st birthday. She is different from the girly girls he has dated in the past. Her family has a long lineage of serving in the military, and her brother had served in Vietnam. She was taught to shoot at an early age and was a great shot. She liked to fish and hunt, and she didn't shy away from getting her hands dirty. Tom felt like he had found a kindred spirit, someone who understood and appreciated him for who he was now.

So, after dating for almost a year, Tom got down on one knee and asked her to marry him. Six months later, he was standing at the altar saying his "I do's."

They moved into the ten-acre homestead his mom and dad had left him. His parents were now living in an RV, touring the county, and enjoying their retirement, but they were always welcome and had a place to stay when they came back home.

Tom was over the moon when Jackie told him she was pregnant. He was excited about the prospect of having a little one running around the house.

On February 1, 1989, Tom got paged to the office of the packing company where he worked. He had a phone call. It was Jackie telling him to hurry home because she was in labor. With his heart racing, Tom clocked out, jumped into his truck, and drove like a bat out of hell toward home. As he drove, his mind raced with thoughts of his future being a dad. He pictured himself playing catch with his son in the front yard, teaching him how to hunt and fish, and watching him grow into a strong and independent young man. Upon arriving home, he raced into the house, grabbed Jackie's overnight bag, and helped her out to the vehicle.

    The road to the hospital seemed to stretch on forever, but Tom refused to let his anxiety get the better of him. As they had pulled up to the hospital entrance, Tom quickly put the truck in park and raced to the passenger door. He helped Jackie out of the truck and held her hand tightly as they made their way inside. A nurse helped Jackie get settled into a wheelchair, and then they all made their way to a private room, where the nurses immediately started to monitor Jackie's contractions. It wasn't long before she was wheeled into the delivery room. Tom was nervous but ready for this moment.

Tom heard the nurse tell Jackie to push one last time before hearing the baby's cry, and the Doctor say, "Congratulations, it's a boy."

Tom felt a surge of emotions, relief, happiness, pride, and his smile was beaming from ear to ear. They had finally started a new chapter in their lives, he thought. One that held the promises of hope, love, and joy.

Chapter 7 "Youth"
February 1, 1999, through September 11, 2001

At ten years of age, Joey starts taking an interest in all things military. He reads everything he can get his hands on about World War II, the Korean War, and Vietnam. He often asks his dad about his time in Nam, but Tom really doesn't want to talk about it and tries to steer the conversation in a different direction. That is why Joey sought out veterans and spent hours listening to their stories. They enjoyed his company and his sincere interest, and he relished being with them.

Joey spends much of his youth in the woods, playing Army and working on his stealth while playing hide-and-go-seek with other kids living nearby. He wears BDU pants, purchased at an Army surplus store, and military-style t-shirts. He loves collecting WWII and Vietnam memorabilia and spends hours searching for the perfect piece to add to his collection in secondhand or surplus stores. He wants to jump out of planes and hence practices climbing trees and jumping out of them.

Joey counts down the days until his 12th birthday and has Tom march him over to the local Civil Air Patrol squadron in their hometown so that he can get signed up. Joey was excited that they would teach him how to fly a plane.

As a parent, the thought of his child serving in the military fills Tom with a sense of unease. But despite his reservations, he can't help but feel proud of Joey's passion for aviation and his desire to serve his country someday.

Although Tom knows the risks that come with military service, he also recognizes the value of the friendships and camaraderie that come with being part of a team. And so even though he doesn't want him to enlist, Tom supports Joey's decision to join the Air Force Auxiliary. Watching him connect with other kids who share his interests and aspirations, Tom knows he is in good company. Joey is happy to be surrounded by those who understand the thrill of flying and the call to serve. Tom is grateful that Joey has found a community where he can explore his passions.

Tom had to admit that CAPS has a good program. They provide youth-scaled, Air Force-themed extracurricular activities. Cadet life for Joey is fun and meaningful, and it is a positive place for him to develop leadership skills while exploring aviation. They gather weekly for a two-hour meeting on one Saturday per month. Joey could not get enough of the week-long encampment over the summer each year. He flourishes in the activities such as rappelling, obstacle courses, firearms training, and the like, which encourages safe, calculated risk-taking objectives in a safe environment.

Tom is home sick in bed on September 11, 2001, when he gets a call from his wife, Jackie, to turn on the TV. He watches in disbelief as the news reports a hijacked flight that has just crashed into the 93rd to 99th floors of the north tower of the world trade center. He sees the smoke billowing out of the building and the chaos in the streets below as he tries to comprehend what is happening. He watches in horror as he sees the second plane come into view and crash into the 77th to 85th floors of the second tower just 17 minutes later at 9:03 am. He feels as if he has been sucker punched in the gut. No, no, no, he keeps repeating in his head. He knows if this were indeed a terrorist act from a foreign land, this means war. His thoughts then shift to his son Joey.

Joey is in Mrs. Smith's science class when there is a knock at the classroom door. She stops her lecture and goes over to open it. After a brief whispered conversation with the assistant principal, she closes the door and turns on the TV. In disbelief, Joey; and his classmates watch as the second plane hits the south tower while the news crew correspondents talk about what has happened or is happening with the other three hijacked planes. There is stone silence in the room as they hear the reporters ask questions about the possibility of going to war. Although Joey has already made his commitment to serve, this act of terrorism just makes his commitment that much stronger.

Chapter 8 "At least we are Friends"
August 12, 2004, through October 27, 2007

Tom's marriage is strained, and although he doesn't want a divorce, he knows Jackie isn't happy with their relationship. While they have so much in common, they just don't seem to click anymore. He knows it is more due to him than it is to her. He knows he is difficult to live with due to his PTSD, nightmares, and demons. There were so many events and get-togethers that she didn't attend because he refused to go, and she didn't want to go alone. She had to carry the load alone so many times because he was going through a meltdown and was drinking more than he should in an attempt to self-medicate and block out the past. So, it didn't surprise him when Jackie came home one day in August and handed him the finalized divorce papers. It was a no-contest divorce as they had already agreed on all the issues, such as marital property, spousal support, division of shared debt, and, most importantly, that they would share 50/50 child custody, visitation, and child support.

At least we are parting as friends and not bitter enemies, he thinks, especially since we both want and need to be involved in our son's life.

When Joey enters High School, he immediately joins their Army JROTC and Raiders programs. He thrives in these physically demanding clubs that teach soldiering skills and allows teams to compete in obstacle courses, rope bridge, and cross-country rescue, a simulation in which a team moves military equipment and casualties as fast as possible.

Many; who join JROTC in High School, come from a lineage of men and women who answered the call to serve this great nation, but almost all of these high school kids have a strong desire to serve in the Armed Forces upon graduation.

Joey and his friends often have these conversations about 'serving after high school, which creates a strong connection among them. A bond that reflects that of soldiers, battle buddies, or small military units. You care for one another, and you support one another.

Throughout high school, Joey continues his involvement in CAPS, JROTC, and the Raiders Program while counting down the days to enlist. He makes recruiters nervous when this 15-year-old kid corners them in the hall to learn more about what enlistments mean, what jobs there are, when can he take the ASVAB, and whether he could have some more swag.

"Let's talk when you're 16", they say, but that doesn't stop Joey from continuing to bug the recruiters every chance he gets.

As high school is coming to a close, Joey is preparing to graduate and has already enlisted to go immediately to BCT and AIT to become an infantryman. Tom is so proud of his son as he watches him walk across the stage to receive his High School diploma. At the same time, it scares him, knowing that soon Joey will leave for boot camp.

The days fly by, and the next thing Tom knows, it is time for Joey to leave for Fort Benning, GA, for both BCT/AIT and Airborne School. Tom relishes the moments when he gets a letter from Joey during basic. It is a very emotional day when he goes and watches his son graduate basic in a traditional and time-honored turning blue ceremony before continuing on to Airborne and acquiring his maroon beret.

Joey keeps in touch through phone calls, emails, and Facebook while stationed at Ft. Bragg, and Tom enjoys hearing and reading about his son's time with 4th BDE, 82ND Airborne. Tom remembers thinking, "Those guys sound crazy," and later would go on to understand that his assessment of those "All-American" guys was so true — they are a different breed of Soldier.

Chapter 9 "Emails Home"
August 19, 2009, through September 21, 2009

From: Joey Johnson

To: Thomas Johnson

Subject: Arrival

Date: August 19, 2009

Hey Dad,

Just wanted to let you know that I made it over here ok, but it was a long plane ride. It was kind of surreal. Being a gunner, I had to carry my 240, which is this machine gun about 4 feet tall that shoots 7.62-millimeter bullets, and my M4 with my 203, which is the grenade launcher strapped to that. It was the whole nine yards, all military, but walking through the airport carrying a machine gun was just unreal. But the crazy part is that we boarded a commercial flight with a stewardess just like we would be going on a flight to anywhere as a civilian.

It was hard to get much sleep as everyone talked smack and hyped up about what was coming. Once we landed, we got off the commercial flight and loaded into some C130s to take us to an Air Force base. That is when it hit me that this was real and not just some cool experience anymore and that I was really going to be fighting in a war.

I love you and hope you are doing well. I promise to write again soon when I have some computer time.

All my love,
Joey

From: Joey Johnson

To: Thomas Johnson

Subject: It's crazy

Date: September 6, 2009

Hey Dad,

We kind of hit the ground running. It is crazy how you feel immortal when you are being shot at and not hit. Sometimes we have to do night travel on a Chinook. It's loud as hell, so you got your headphones on. But then you start seeing sparks. There are sparks everywhere along the whole bottom of the Chinook. It's the Taliban shooting up at the Chinook you are in, but because it's armor-plated, you know they won't be able to take it down with an AK 47. But it is wild to see the flicker of the gunfire and the sparks, so you know they are shooting at us. And while you know that they might as well be using a BB gun at that point, you still wonder if they have something more than just the AK 47s. You kind of don't want to acknowledge that they could have something more, and you are the target. Then when you finally land, you're like, WOW, that just got real.

I suppose if I am ever hit and survive, I might not feel immortal anymore. I hope I never have to find out if I am right or not on that thought.

I have started to learn that we don't always succeed in our missions, but we learn from them. We adapt so that the next time when the Taliban brings the fight to our door, they will come to understand that it's not about revenge. It is about avenging and reckoning.

I love you and miss you. I will email again when I get some more computer time.

All my love,
Joey

From: Joey Johnson
To: Thomas Johnson
Subject: Devastated
Date: September 21, 2009

Hey Dad,

It is with a heavy heart that I write this. Two days ago marked one month since we left home, but yesterday was one of the hardest days of my life. Around 0600, my very good friend Billy was severely injured, and my best friend Corey was killed. Both were brothers to me. Corey was only 20, just like me.

Corey, Billy, and I were in Civil Air Patrol and used to compete against each other. We met through joint training and community events that our squadrons did together. As we all approached high school, we were able to compete against one another in our Army JROTC programs. We were on competing Raider teams as well. We were all cut from the same cloth. Our circle was big but also very small. We all enjoyed JROTC, but a few of us had already committed to serving. Corey, Billy, and I all wanted to join the infantry. Reflecting back, on what I know of Corey, we both had a desire not just to serve but also to have a purpose and be a part of something greater.

Dad, Corey was so funny, and man, could he sing. He just had a way of lifting everyone's spirits when things were down. He was the first KIA in our unit in this war, and make no mistake, war it is. I couldn't tell you about him until after his family had been notified. At 1600 today, the memorial service took place. The most difficult part was when his First Sergeant called the final roll. He called the names of each squad member, and each answered in turn. Then Corey's name was called once, no response. Twice, no response. A third time, no response. I knew there would be no response, and it just killed me inside. How I wanted to hear him call out when his name was called. Then TAPS began to play, accompanied by a 21-gun volley. We were then allowed to file by his helmet atop his rifle, dog tags hanging from it, and all of this behind his boots with a picture of him beside them. They allowed us, row by row, to approach and turn to his equipment to render a final salute. Some of us pulled off patches and placed them in the boots. Others put in coins or other tokens as a way to honor him. I saw a few, who knew him well, break down briefly but as soon as we were told our time was up, soldier mode came back over each and every one of us as we filed back into formation.

My mind keeps going back to the incident. We were out on a combat mission and came under fire. I was in the front Humvee of the four. Corey and Billy were in the last Humvee. Their driver tried to miss what he thought was an IED in the road, yanking the steering wheel to the left. He lost control, and the Humvee started to swerve from side to side. I saw it flip and start to roll. Dad, it rolled three times before coming to rest on its side. Corey had been up top in the turret and couldn't get down inside fast enough. The edges of the turret acted like a guillotine chopping off one of his arms and severing a leg as it flipped. The doors flew off, and those inside got thrown out and had severe injuries but were still alive and medevacked out. Corey was still breathing when I got to him, but I think it was only because his body didn't know he was dead. Several were working on getting tourniquets on his upper right arm by his shoulder and on his left leg right below the knee. I looked around and saw his arm over by the side of the road. I went over and picked it up. While waiting for the chopper to land, I laid his arm on his chest. I didn't know what else to do. Billy was in pretty bad shape, as were the others, and they will probably end up being medically discharged due to their injuries, but at least they are still alive.

I am so angry as this didn't have to happen! The Humvees we had to use were in really bad shape. We had no radio communication between the vehicles, and most of them had no brakes. The one Corey was in had only three brake pads, two of which were cracked. All three pads were less than one millimeter thick. That isn't thick enough to stop a car, let alone a heavy combat vehicle. I just don't understand why our country is sending millions of dollars in aid to other countries and yet unwilling to ensure our own military has adequate equipment in a war zone. There is talk around the FOB that they may try to court-martial the Sergeant or Lieutenant for this, but it isn't their fault they have to make do with what equipment we have at the FOB. It just pisses me off!

This is probably harder for you to read than it was for me to write, but I know you understand from your time in Nam. There are some things I have been putting off saying, something I can no longer do. I am a SOLDIER. I am sworn to protect and defend, and I will do that until my last breath, be it in the military or after, as this is my calling. I have no desire to die, but it is a price I am willing to pay for my country in the name of freedom. I love you all more than life itself, so I am here.

Zabul is a cesspool of insurgents. They will give us no piece. Daily we bring the fight to their door. Before yesterday, even though we were here, it still didn't feel real. It felt like we were shooting at "pop-up targets" that couldn't hit back. Now they are hitting back. But they screwed up. Our innocence is gone. We will fight with honor, obey the laws of war, and go out of our way to help the innocent, but there will be no mercy for those who rise up against us. For them, hell will be unleashed.

I am sorry that these things needed to be said. You needed to know, in case they ever call my final roll, I love and miss you very much. If you talk to Mom, please tell her I love and miss her too but don't share this email with her. I don't want her to worry any more than I know she already does. I WILL be coming home. Just 11 more months to go.

All my love,
Joey

Chapter 10 "Coming Home"
July 22, 2010, through October 17, 2011

From: Joey Johnson
To: Thomas Johnson
Subject: Coming Home
Date: July 22, 2010

Hey Dad,

I am so glad that I will be coming home soon. Yesterday was crazy. I was out as a gunner. I trust my truck commander as he is the controller of everything that happens in our vehicle. So that means I don't shoot or do anything without his guidance. I know you understand…. how you have that trust back and forth. But yesterday, it was, "Sir, I got a kid. I think he has a gun. Permission to shoot." And my Staff Sergeant, he's like, "Is it a true P ID (positive identification)?" and pretty much gave me the clear to fire as long as I had a P ID that this kid truly had a weapon.

I won't lie, Dad. My heart was racing as I racked the 50 cal and was ready to fire that warning shot when I noticed the AK 47 the kid was holding was a toy. I tell you I about passed out. I almost killed this kid because he had a toy AK-47!!!

This was one of those moments of holy shit!! This is the real world and not a video game. This is where decisions, on a 20-year-old level, have life and death consequences on children, and it was just like… Oh Shit!

It was hard, you know? I kept thinking about how close I was to pulling the trigger. And it would have been the wrong choice. Thankfully, I realized in time that the kid wasn't really pointing the gun at us or anything in particular but was just holding it.

How I wanted to go find and ask that kid's parents, "What were you thinking to allow your child to have a realistic toy AK-47 to play with when you know that the military is going through here and they are going to shoot if they see someone with a weapon."

I don't understand, Dad, where they can get a toy that looks so real. And it sucks that we can't always tell what is real and what isn't real. Especially when they use kids to get close to us to cause harm. Just the other day, a 7- or 8-year-old kid threw an RKG-3 (which is a Russian-made grenade shaped like a beer bottle that, when it heats up and blows, causes the shape of the grenade to become that of a spear and it'll go straight through armor like butter) at one of the armored vehicles we were in and it almost killed the medic.

I am still trying to wrap my brain around it all. How can parents let their kids do that? How kids can be recruited and brainwashed to carry out an attack. Is it because these kids have grown up with these sights of death and destruction? Is war just their train of thought? Are they just living out that fantasy of wanting to serve, as many kids in America do, but with different worldly consequences?

Don't get me wrong; I still love being in the Army. I just don't always like what I have to do, and the decisions I have to make in a split second. That can be a heavy weight to bear.

Well, I must go for now, but I look forward to getting one of your hugs soon. And I am also looking forward to going fishing with you.

Love always,
Joey

NOVEMBER 1, 2010

Joey was glad to be home and looking forward to seeing Billy. They had talked several times on the phone, but this was the first time since returning from Afghanistan that they could meet in person. Billy still had visible scars on his arms and was walking with a limp due to the leg injury.

"Hey Billy," Joey said as he hugged him. "How are you doing, man?"

"Joey, it's so great seeing you," Billy replied. "Can't lie; it sucked being hospitalized while you guys were still over there. I so wanted to be there with you. But it wasn't meant to be. They are going to be medically discharging me soon. This is just not the way I wanted to go out, you know? I was planning on doing my 20 and then getting out. What can I say? It's just not how I had it planned."

"Billy, you know it's weird being back. I didn't realize how vivid the colors are here. Everything is so pastel over there, grays, browns, greens, mauves. Here it is reds, oranges, pinks, yellow, and blues. And marketing signs… now it seems like we over market with colors."

"Yeah, I know what you mean, Joey. I had a hard time eating when I got back. Eating anything salted made me sick. I guess it was because we got used to not having it in our diet."

"And the butter and sugar." Joey said, "I tried eating some pancakes right when I returned since it was one of my favorite meals, and I couldn't eat them because they tasted disgusting. All I could taste was the butter. I took the butter off and then tasted the butter they cooked it in, and the syrup was like eating sugar. It was too sweet, and it was making me gag."

"Joey, to tell ya the truth… it's been hard since I got out of the hospital. Physically I know I am about as good as I will get. I can live with that. What I am having problems with is trying to fit back in. I was so used to being around 38 people who knew my ins and outs, and I knew theirs. You get to know their bad days and good days. Their smells and their personalities. What triggers them, and what doesn't? You develop this very tight-knit family, and then, suddenly, you get thrown into the fish tank of regular society. And everybody seems to be in your face. That's when I start getting that anxiety… you know?"

"Yeah, I get it.' Joey commiserated. "It's weird how fast-paced everyone seems to be. I sometimes feel like I am on a two-mile-an-hour pace while everyone else is going one hundred miles an hour around you."

"Yes," replied Billy. "Like you grew up on some midwestern farm in a hick one-stop light small town, and then you were just transported to the Vegas strip or downtown New York City in a blink of an eye. Trying to figure it out. Trying to navigate your way back so you don't feel uncomfortable. You just want to stick with your core group because it is safe. They get you."

"I know what you mean, Billy. I hated losing our peer group because some didn't make it home, got medevacked out, got stationed at other places, or were getting out right after returning. Next thing you know, it seems it's down to just you. You start getting ranked, and then you get the FNGs (fucking new guys) in your unit. And it's like, wow, now I am one step up. Now you have 30 new people from all walks of life you don't know. You are thrust into a leadership position. You start thinking, what is my responsibility in training these new privates? Trying to rationalize my and their well-being. Knowing that when we get deployed again, I will have to count on these FNGs that are not as seasoned as being on a battlefield or the cherries which have not been deployed yet. But in doing so, you kind of realize that the best way to avoid that thought is to just think about training."

"How is training going? Billy asked.

"Well, I have to say one thing. While we always pick on the Marines, I must give them their props. They do have their shit together when it comes to providing schooling. Yes, sir, they do know how to do school. Probably one of the coolest ones I did, was being shuttled in with a chinook in the middle of the mountains in California. It was a five-day crash course on survival in the cold climate and dealing with rappelling, knot tying, and evacuating through a helicopter where you can't get vehicles in and all your other ins and outs. It's like, here's how to skin a rabbit. Here's how to cook a rabbit. Here's how to provide safety for yourself. Here's how to read and use your map and other techniques. And then it was like… any questions? Nope? Ok, gear up, and then we are dropped into the middle of nowhere. We had a 60-mile course to go through, and everything we needed was out there, like water. While we did carry in some food, we also had drops with resupply points, as we had on missions. And then the Marines would provide the opposing force. We would have MILES gear like some awesome giant laser tag game where you have all these receptors all over your body. Then you have your weapon system with a blank flash adapter and a laser trigger. So, you would get into all these ambush points. We'd try to get water and then realize they had the water cut off. Then we'd go another day without water. And we had to figure out all the maneuverability around it. Yep, the Marines do have the training down for sure. But you know what I find strange? I thought leadership would be a fun position, but in many ways, it's not. Now the pressure is on you. You have to be that figure that is calm and counted on. To be the one who makes the right decisions. Do not show fear because you want them not to be afraid. And if I am not that figure, then there will be problems."

Time passed quickly as Joey and Billy continued to reminisce about the past, their time serving together, and their thoughts on the future. All too soon, they realized that they needed to say their goodbyes. They stood and grasped each other's hand, pulled themselves into each other, and then slapped each other on the back. "Man... so glad to see you again," Joey mumbled. "Yeah, I know. Been too long," replied Billy. And with that, they turned and walked to their cars.

OCTOBER 17, 2011

Tom and Joey were wrapping up their day fishing along the banks of the river when Joey broke the silence. "Dad, it's hard to believe I will return to Afghanistan soon. Seems like I just got back."

"Joey, I'm not going to lie. I held my breath the whole time you were there. I never thought much about how my dad felt when I was in Nam, but if it was anything like what I went through, he worried. He worried a lot. I mean, you know that some of them don't make it home. Yet, you can't think that way, as it will eat you up inside. You have to remain positive. But I must admit that I was really worried about how you would be once you got home. I know how it messed me up, and I didn't want that for you."

"It definitely changes you," replied Joey.

"Son, I know I don't say it often enough, but I am so proud of you. And I love you."

"I love you too, Dad."

Chapter 11 "COP Zerok"
November 14, 2011, through December 21, 2011

From: Joey Johnson
To: Thomas Johnson
Subject: COP Zerok
Date: November 14, 2011

Hey Dad,

I just got to Afghanistan, and let me tell you, it was a wild ride. I am leading a mortar team this time, which is a big change from being a gunner during my last deployment.

When we landed at COP Zerok, it was a crazy touch-and-go maneuver. We were off the helicopter in the blink of an eye. The whole landing process only took 30 seconds, and the helicopter didn't even touch the ground! We had to do it that way to avoid becoming a target for the enemy. It was intense, to say the least.

As soon as we got off the helicopter, a few guys met us with big smiles on their faces, saying, "Welcome to COP Zerok!" But then, we started taking rocket fire. I mean, talk about a wild welcome party! The guys there before us had a sign that said, "Mortar free for 00 days," which pretty much summed up the security situation.

Despite the attack, everyone was friendly and welcoming. It was almost surreal. We quickly reached a building to figure out our next steps. It wasn't even a "let's get to the bunker and stay safe" situation. It was more like, "Let's get inside so we can plan our next move."

The commander of the unit briefed me on the situation. We were in a hostile area and needed to defend the outpost while maintaining control of the surrounding area. There were a couple of approaches we could take, and we needed to make a decision quickly.

My team and I assessed the situation and came up with a plan. We took over the mortar positions and provided cover fire while the infantry units secured the perimeter. The battle was fierce and lasted for hours, but we held our ground and eventually emerged victorious. However, it was not without significant casualties.

Looking back on the experience, I'm proud of what we accomplished. We were able to work together to defend our position and push back the enemy. It was a sobering reminder of the dangers of war and a testament to the bravery and resilience of the soldiers who fought it.

Anyway, I just wanted to share my experience with you. I promise to write again soon when I can. Take care!

Miss you and love you!
Love always,
Joey

From: Billy
To: Joey
Subject: Updates
Date: November 18, 2011

    Hellooooooo Joey!

    It's been a while since I last wrote. Just wanted to update you on what was happening. The Army has medically discharged me, and I have found a place to land. Very strange being out. I feel like I have lost my tribe, and now I am the sole survivor adrift on a raft in the middle of the ocean, and the sharks are circling. The only upside so far is that I will start to train soon with my new service dog. I am looking forward to it. It will be great having someone in my life that has my back.

    Also, I won't be alone in my studio apartment with nothing to do. It's hard sometimes to keep the demons at bay when you have too much time.

    Hope to hear from you soon, bro!
    Billy

From: Joey
To: Billy
Subject: Ambushed
Date: November 21, 2011

Hey Billy,

It's been quite a wild ride, to say the least. It's funny how all the training we've done is now something we get to put into action. We've been on missions where we meet with local villagers, and sometimes we have to cordon off the area for safety purposes. Other times, we go on village raids in search of high-value targets.

Unfortunately, things can escalate pretty quickly when we cross certain lines. It's like there's this invisible boundary that once we pass, we know it's game on. Troops in contact, here we come. If we need support, we'll radio in for close air support, and within seconds, we'll have two F16s on station ready to drop bombs if necessary. And if we need something with a little more oomph, we'll call in the a-10 Warthogs.

Speaking of which, we were out on patrol the other day and got ambushed. We were in a really low spot and surrounded by mountains. It was like something out of a movie. We were getting hit from all sides by machine gunfire and rockets. It was nuts. We had to low crawl to fighting positions, and then we called in the A-10s. We call them the "Kraken" because they're the beast of the sky. Even though this thing is huge and slow, but it packs a serious punch. It's got a 35-millimeter grenade launcher that unleashes a ridiculous number of rounds per second. Remember how is sounds when it fires, "rrrrrrrrraaaaaaaaaaa," and then you hear "tttttttttttttttt" as it unleashes complete and utter destruction. It's just carnage, man. The smell of death was everywhere.

But we had a job to do, so we went in and surveyed the POO (Point Of Origin) sights to see where all the enemy contact was coming from and where all the explosives were. We also checked to see if there were any survivors and if we could capture anyone or confiscate any equipment. It was snipers, small arms fire, and rockets. The whole nine yards.

So, that pretty much sums up our day-to-day. We're always on our A-game, and we've had no casualties so far. But, man, do I wish you were here with us.

Miss you, bro.
Take care,
Joey

From: Joey Johnson
To: Thomas Johnson
Subject: COP Zerok
Date: November 22, 2011

Hey Dad,

Some days out here can be pretty rough. We have to go on twenty-four-hour walks sometimes, where we would walk for 12 hours and then sit and wait at an ambush point for whatever might come our way. Other times, we'd stay overnight in preparation for the next day's mission. Each person in the platoon carries two heavy mortar rounds, and on top of that, the belt-fed machine gunners carry belts of ammo, and squad leaders and platoon leaders carry belts of ammo too. And let's not forget our magazines, each of us carrying seven to eight-round magazines. It's a lot to carry, especially during a long walk.

Unfortunately, sometimes our missions get cut short. We could be several hours into our walk when we get ambushed and end up expending all of our ammo there. Then we don't have the necessary equipment or ammunition to complete our planned mission. The enemy always wants to stop us before achieving our objective.

It's a constant state of being on guard. You start automatically going into that mindset of having Troops in Contact. And when the mission is done, everyone is just exhausted. Totally spent. You're mentally and physically drained and hoping nothing else happens because you just want to return to the safety of the COP. You're low on ammo, food, and energy, mentally exhausted, and covered with sweat from head to toe, with bleeding feet. We walk back for hours and finally see the American flag on the ridge line. It's the endpoint, home, safety, food, resupply, friends, and everything we need. Seeing the flag is such a relieving visual, representing our freedom, our safety and our unity.

Sometimes I wish those disrespecting our flag could experience just one day in our boots. Then they just might understand the unifying source it is and what it truly means. That it symbolizes unity regardless of background, sex, religion, race, or sexual preference. We're all Americans; we're family. It's just powerful!

Anyway, I guess I'll get off my soapbox now.

Miss you, Dad, and your hugs too!

Love always,

Joey

P.S. If you send me a care package, please send me lots of beef jerky!

From: Joey
To: Billy
Subject: Thanks
Date: December 2, 2011

Hey Billy,

Thanks for the Thanksgiving wishes! To be honest, it was just another day in this shit-hole. I don't think anyone on this base even felt it was a holiday. But hey, at least we got a decent meal out of it.

I hear you on not missing Afghanistan. It's been a tough deployment so far, and trying to envision an end in sight is hard. I'm taking it one day at a time, trying just to focus on the mission.

Speaking of the future, I've been thinking a lot about what I want to do when I get out of here. The idea of jumping back into civilian life is both exciting and intimidating. I've been considering using my GI bill to go back to College and major in Political Science. It's a subject that's always fascinated me, and maybe I can make some sense of the crazy political landscape we're living in these days.

Love ya Bro!
Joey

P.S. SEND ME JERKY!!!

From: Billy
To: Joey
Subject: Good news
Date: December 21, 2011

Hellooooooo Joey!

Great to hear you are thinking about using your GI Bill and going to College when you get out. Maybe I could use my GI Bill and go too. I have been thinking I would like to get a degree in Animal Behavior. We could room together. That would be so awesome!!!!

This reminds me that I wanted to let you know that I have just completed the training with my service dog. I cannot begin to tell you how cool it is. I don't know how to explain it, but he's like family to me already. His name is Six. Told you he would have my back!!

Keep your head down and write again soon!
Love ya Bro!
Billy

Chapter 12 "First Impressions"
December 31, 2011

Tom drives into the Piggly Wiggly parking lot to pick up a few more items for his New Year's Eve get-together. He doesn't like the crowds nor the sound of the fireworks, so every year, he invites between 5 and 8 guys to come for a cookout, and they usually ring in the New Year sitting around a fire pit.

His property is far enough away from town that they don't hear the noise but close enough that they can still see the beauty of the fireworks show the town puts on each year. It was a perfect way to bring in the new year. Some guys bring their wives, dates, or friends, and some come solo. Since Tom's divorce, he has always been solo.

Tom finds a parking space and parks next to a blue van. Just as he is about to get out, he notices a nice-looking lady with dark brown hair starting to gray come around the back of the van carrying two brown paper bags of groceries.

As she tries to open the sliding side door, one of the bags breaks open, and groceries start falling to the ground.

"Oh, that is just lovely," he hears her say in exasperation. Tom can't help but chuckle as he watches her struggle to open the door. *A damsel in distress,* he thinks as he gets out of his truck. "Here, let me help you," Tom says as he takes the one bag out of her arms so she can open the door unencumbered. "Thank you," Annie replies. "I appreciate the help."

After placing the one bag inside the van, Annie turns to pick up the grocery items that have fallen. Tom hears her mumble, "Guess it will be McDonald's for dinner," as she picks up the chicken wings scattered everywhere on the asphalt. Tom helps pick up the oranges that have rolled under his truck as he asks, "You don't have plans for tonight?"

"No, not really." She replies. "I have an invitation to go to a party, but I am not sure I want to go."

"Why not?" Tom asks inquisitively.

"Oh… I don't know. Sometimes I just prefer to ring in the new year with my dog. It is a lot easier, and I don't feel awkward kissing someone I don't really know."

"Yeah… I know what you mean." Tom replies as he finishes helping Annie pick up the rest of her groceries.

He couldn't help noticing how pretty she was. Petite and curvy with deep blue eyes. He felt some electricity in the air as he introduces himself.

"Hell of a way to meet, but I'm Tom. You?"

"Annie," she says, extending her hand to shake his. "And thank you for helping me pick up my groceries."

Tom can feel his pulse race as their hands embrace in a handshake. "You're welcome. The least I could do... I don't mind helping a damsel in distress occasionally."

"Well, thank you, Mr. Knight in shining armor." She said in a sexy tone. "It's not often I need to be rescued, but I appreciate it when it happens." With that, Annie slowly pulls her hand away from his. "Have a great New Year's Eve, and wishing you a fantastic new year." She says as she opens her van's driver's side door and hops inside. "You too!" replies Tom as he heads towards the entrance of the Piggly Wiggly.

Tom couldn't get Annie out of his mind as he walked the isles looking for the items he needed. He was kicking himself for not asking her to come to his party.

After paying for his groceries, he returned to his truck and headed home. His mind kept drifting off to Annie. There was just something about her. *I should have at least asked for her number*, he thought. Oh well… probably better this way since he wasn't good in relationships.

After arriving back at the homestead, Tom starts preparing for the evening. He starts by seasoning the ribeye steaks and preparing the vegetable kabobs for the grill. The salad was already tossed and, in the refrigerator, along with the key lime pies. Satisfied that most of the prep work for the party is done, he meanders over to his fully stocked bar and pours himself a drink. Might as well take it easy until the guests arrive, he concludes to himself.

At around 5:00 pm, he steps outside to the patio and lights up the charcoal briquets in the grill. It isn't long after that that the first guests begin to show up.

"Hey Marshall, it's good to see you," Tom says as he steps back to let his friend enter. "Good seeing you too, Tom," he replies. "Where should I put this beer?" "Man, you should know the drill by now. In the bar room fridge," Tom states. "Oh, and can you greet the rest of the guests as they arrive for me? I need to get the steaks and veggies on the fire." "Sure thing. I got it covered." Marshall responds. "You go do your magic on the grill!"

Tom grabs the plate of steaks and the platter of vegetable kabobs and heads out the back door to the patio area where the grill is located.

As he is cooking, more and more of his friends arrive. They know the drill. Help themselves to a drink and make themselves at home. Most would meander out to the covered patio and find a comfortable chair or head over to the pool table or the dart board. Soon it is a party with laughter, music, and a comfortable amount of his peers talking smack or challenging each other to a game. This is his tribe. He feels safe with them.

"This ribeye steak is pretty good." Tom overhears a girl saying to one of his friends. Tom turns around to flaunt his cooking skills and is dumb-struck to see that the girl is Annie. He could not have mistaken her for anyone else. Her curvy and petite figure, those deep blue eyes and shoulder length, slightly curly, dark brown hair with beautiful shades of gray throughout.

"Well, if it isn't the damsel in distress," Tom calls out, making sure not to come off too excited. Nonchalantly he leaves the grill to walk up to her and his friend Jason. Annie recognizes him immediately.

"So, this is the party you didn't want to go to? Tom chided.

Annie coyly puts a strand of hair behind her ear. "If I had known it was your party, I might have thought otherwise," she teasingly replied.

Noticing her attempt to flirt, Tom turned to his friend and asked, "So, how long have the two of you been dating?"

"What? No. She's my cousin," Jason replies. "But how do you two know each other?"

Oddly satisfied by the answer, Tom chuckled, "Oh, my bad. Well, we kind of met earlier today in a parking lot over a bag of runaway groceries. I asked her if she had plans for tonight, and she told me she had a date with her dog!"

"Anyway, what changed your mind?" Tom asks Annie, referring to their previous conversation in the Piggly Wiggly.

"Eating McDonald's alone in my apartment with only my dog on New Year's Eve sounded too sad, even for me," Annie replied.

Tom chuckles and asks if she would like to help him finish cooking the last few steaks and kabobs so that they can continue getting to know each other while he completes his grill master duties.

They sit together through dinner, enjoying each other's company. Then came the time, right before dessert, when Tom raised his glass for the traditional New Year's Eve toast.

"Here is to my friends, who are my bond family. Thank you for being in my life. And, here is to the guests of my tribe, who must be special too, or you probably would not be in their lives. To everyone here, may the new year be good to you, bringing in much love, peace, and joy. Cheers!" With that, they all raised their glasses and clinked them to the glasses of the friends sitting around them. Tom clinked his glass first with his friends and lastly with Annie. Looking into her eyes, he couldn't help but wonder what this new year would bring.

After dinner, Annie helped him with cleanup, and then they found a comfortable spot on the patio to watch the city's fireworks display light up the night. Time passed so fast that it wasn't long before everyone was eagerly getting ready to start the countdown. Tom popped the champagne bottles and started filling up the glasses as Annie was handing them out. He watched as the couples rushed over to their partners for a kiss while the singles raised a toast as they began counting down, starting at 10.

3..2..1.. Tom and Annie looked at each other, and without a word, they both took a step toward each other and kissed. After, what felt like heaven for Tom, they slowly took a step back. Tom can see a blush creep up

Annie's cheek but doesn't comment, guessing he might be looking the same.

"Is there any chance I can get your number?" Tom asks to break the silence.

"Sure," Annie says.

Just like that, they both spent this New Year's Eve totally opposite of what they had envisioned it to be.

CHAPTER 13 "XinHua"
August 17, 2012

From: Billy

To: Joey

Subject: CALL ME ASAP! EMERGENCY!

Date: August 17, 2012

    Joey,

    This is an emergency!!!

    Give me a call as soon as you can after getting this email. XinHua (pronounced Shin-Wa) just texted me this note:

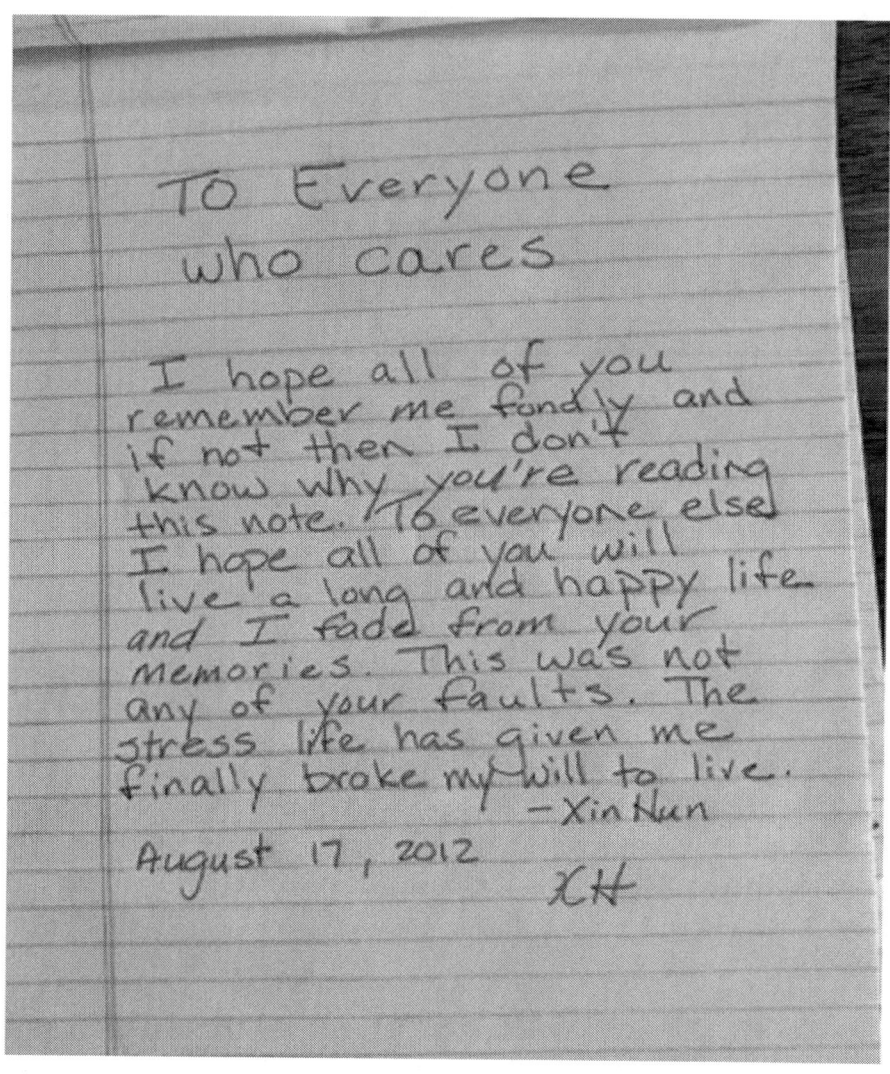

Billy could see by the caller's I.D. that Joey was calling, and he snatched up the phone to answer.

"Billy, what is fuck is going on? When did XinHua text you? Do you know where he is? Is he ok?"

"Joey, it's too late. By the time we were able to get someone from his base to check on him, he was dead. I don't get it. I just spoke with him the other day, and he seemed fine. I feel like this is my fault because I should have noticed something... but I didn't. I keep thinking back to our conversation, and I don't recall anything he said that made me think he was suicidal. I mean, he was always so happy. You know? He was the only one of us who went on to serve in the Air Force after getting out of Civil Air Patrol. Always saying he was living the dream!"

"I know," Joey replied. "Do you remember him telling us about his life? He overcame so much."

"Yeah," Billy said, "I remember him telling us how his birth father had left him on the steps of the Chinese police department when he was only 5 and told him to wait there for him, but he never returned. How the police gave him to a very poor orphanage in Sozhou, China, just west of Shanghai. How his diet consisted of a cup of rice and a boiled egg every day. And when he arrived in the U.S. after being adopted at the age of 8, he weighed about 45 pounds."

"I remember him telling us how he didn't speak any English when he got adopted and moved here," Joey replied. "How almost every day, after his dad got home from work, they would sit in the driveway, and how his "Beh bah" (the word for daddy in Chinese) would point to an object, a tree, a flower, an ant, a bee, a bird, an airplane, whatever came across their path, and his dad would write the word in English with chalk on the driveway and say the word, and then XinHua would repeat the word in English and then write it in Chinese next to it. And, how by sundown the driveway would be covered with all the beauty that surrounded them only to be hosed off that evening in preparation for the next day." Joey reminisced, "You know, it always amazed me that XinHua said he had a pretty good grasp of the English language after only about six weeks of doing that with his dad."

"Yep, he was one smart dude, alright, but the one thing he could never quite grasp was sarcasm." Billy chuckled.

"OMG… it was hilarious!" Joey chimed in. "Always asking why we said certain things a certain way. And then, when he would try using it on girls to impress them, it would usually fall flat. That would just crack me up!"

Suddenly the reality of their friend being gone hit them, and the conversation turned solemn.

"I just can't believe he is gone." Billy choked out as he tried to hold back the tears.

"I know," replied Joey. "Are you going to try and attend the funeral?"

"I don't know, Joey. I mean… I want to, but I am afraid to. I am afraid his mom and dad will hate me because I am still here, and XinHua is not. Hate me because I didn't stop it somehow. That I didn't notice anything was wrong. I mean, we are trained to see this sort of thing before it happens, but I didn't see this coming. How can I say I was his friend when I obviously didn't know he was hurting and contemplating taking his own life? What kind of friend is that?"

Before Joey could answer, Billy heard the sirens going off, and Joey say, "Gotta go bro."

"Keep your head down, brother!" Billy replied right before he heard the click of the call ending.

CHAPTER 14 "The Funeral"
August 26, 2012

A memorial service was held for XinHua at Joint Base Andrews, presided by Lt Col Frank Bellows. Billy was seated in the back row with Six at his feet. He watched as the family was escorted to the front row of the chapel. He was a little surprised as to how few people besides the family that was there. The Lt Col talked of XinHua's many accomplishments, including a congressional citation for the work he did in updating the base library. He went on to say that XinHua was one test away from being promoted to Staff Sergeant, which would have promoted him to intelligence.

Then Airman Campbell took to the podium while choking back tears. He said if it hadn't been for the tutoring, he received from XinHua, he would never have made his last promotion. The whole time during the service, there was a big screen that showed pictures of

XinHua from when he was a kid to the present time. Some of the pictures Billy recognized from a few CAPS events that they had all been at while in High School.

In the end, the Lt Col. turned it over to a Chaplain who said a prayer and asked the family members to please come to the front of the chapel and receive the condolences from some of those in his squadron. That's when Billy noticed, while he had been sitting there listening to the L.T. Col and the Chaplin, that what seemed like the entire base had quietly moved into the chapel. The line of Airmen seemed to go on for the better part of an hour as they paid their respects to the family. Many were in tears themselves, and Billy overheard several say, "We are trained to see this sort of thing before it happens, but nobody saw this coming." Billy agreed. He sure didn't see it coming, and he couldn't stop feeling guilty. What had he not seen or heard? What had he overlooked? Surely this was his fault somehow. Finally, Billy got up the courage and made his way up front to where the family stood. He didn't know what to say.

As Billy approached XinHua's dad, he heard him ask, "So how did you know my son?"

Billy replied, "I served in CAPS at the same time as XinHua. Although we were in different squadrons and competed against each other, we got to be good friends. XinHua always used to tell us about how his *"Beh bah"* taught him how to read, write and speak English. How he was so fortunate to be in America and living with a family who loved him."

XinHua's dad, with tears streaming down his face, reached out and embraced Billy in his arms. "Thank you for sharing that with me," he whispered in Billy's ear.

Billy started to cry and choked out, "I am so, so sorry. I should have seen something. Done something. I feel like I failed him. Please forgive me."

"There is nothing to forgive. It's not your fault," XinHua's dad softly replied.

Billy left the chapel and followed the family to the funeral home where XinHua had been laid in a casket for viewing. It was hard to see his friend lying there in full military dress. Hard knowing it would be the last time he would see him other than in pictures. Hard to wrap his head around the death of another friend, and he wasn't sure he could bear much more.

CHAPTER 15 "War is Hell"
October 19, 2012 through October 30, 2012

The day started as most days did at the COP, but on this day, they were expecting the General to arrive at 1200. When the General didn't show up, everyone went back to what they were doing. Some of them made their way back to the buildings by the mortar pit area, where they could relax and play a video game or two. The buildings were fortified with barriers and had barriers all around them with entrance points to the rooms.

At 1330 an incoming rocket came in and hit the building where Joey and a few others were playing Call of Duty. Tyson had just made his way out the door when the rocket exploded, and it killed him instantly. Dominic, the medic, came running to provide aid but quickly ascertained that there wasn't anything that he could do since there wasn't much left of Tyson's body. Next, he made his way into the building to see if he could save anyone inside. Dominic saw Joey lying in a fetal position. He quickly knelt down and rolled him over. Looking him over, Dominic didn't even know where to start. It was shrapnel from head to toe. Joey had obvious chest wounds and was bleeding out. There was brain matter everywhere. There were pieces of his equipment infused into his skin, and it was one of the most horrifying things Dominic had ever seen.

He was dumbfounded. There's no training for this kind of devastation, he thought. There's no training that can ever prepare anyone for that kind of carnage. Dominic yelled for someone to get on the radio to get medics en route.

At this point, the smoke was just starting to clear, and he was trying to assess for more casualties. Luckily, the others in the room were far enough away from the blast that they were not mortally wounded.

He could hear someone yelling, "What the hell just happened?" as they came running into the room to help provide assistance. It was obvious that several had been knocked across the room by the blast and lay unconscious. Smoke was still going everywhere, along with dust and soot. You could hear everyone choking on it among the sounds of moaning by those who were injured. It was scary as hell as they tried getting those injured on stretchers and moving them to the aid station while they waited for the choppers.

Suddenly, more rockets started coming in and exploding all around them. Immediately they dispersed as they found their way into fighting positions so they could start shooting mortar rounds back towards the location the rockets had come from.

Communicating by radio, they quickly determined the grid location of the incoming rockets and requested air support.

Those not injured come running out, not sure what just happened, trying to take it all in and assess the damage.

Controlling fire so the bird could land with the trauma unit was one of the top priorities. Upon landing, the trauma unit wastes no time attending to the injured. Although Joey was missing brain matter, his body didn't realize he was dead as he was still breathing. The medics began working on Joey even though he was not talking or coherent. With speed and precision, never giving up, they attended to each injured soldier. If they could get that heart started again, they would. If they can get them breathing again, they will. No one will die on their watch if they can help it as they load the bird with the wounded and take off.

At 9:26 a.m., Tom received a knock at his door. He opened it to find a Chaplain and an Army Major from the base standing on his porch. Before he could even comprehend what was going on, he saw the Chaplain pull out a piece of paper and read it out loud in a somber voice, "The Secretary of the Army has asked me to express his deep regret that your son Joey died due to indirect small arms, rocket and mortar fire at COP

Zerok, Afghanistan, on 19 October, 2012. The Army is conducting an investigation into the death of your son. When the investigation is complete, you will be offered the opportunity to receive a copy of the investigation. The Secretary extends his deepest sympathy to you and your family in your tragic loss. An Army casualty assistance officer will contact you shortly. In the meantime, if you have any questions or require assistance, please contact our regional representative at 1-800-557-xxxx."

The reality of it all was finally sinking in as Tom fell to his knees. He didn't remember much after that. It was as if his mind and body were frozen in time. He knew he was asking questions, and they were answering them, but it wasn't sinking into his brain.

The next morning Tom boarded a plane to Dover. He wanted to be there when his son's body came back to U.S. soil after deploying to Afghanistan. He didn't just want to be there; he had to be there. Maybe it was because he felt that if he saw his flag-draped casket, he could finally accept that Joey had really died.

Upon arrival, Tom was driven to a hotel located near the Air Force base. He was instructed to drop off his luggage in his room and then go to a small conference room to meet with more military personnel. Upon entering the conference room, Tom saw his ex-wife, Jackie standing there talking with someone in uniform. Tom could tell she had been crying, and he walked over and gave her a hug. He could feel her start to shudder as the tears welled up in both their eyes. Tom was glad they had remained friends all these years after the divorce. It was making this a little easier to bear. They were immediately inundated with forms that they had to sign. There were a lot of decisions that had to be made. Did they want to allow the press to be present when his coffin was transported from the plane? Did they want the autopsy results? If they chose not to receive them, they would never be able to get them.

They were informed that they would be taken to a special area to view the transfer of the flag-draped coffin from the plane to the hearse. They also were told that they would not be able to see the body or touch the casket.

Tom remembers standing on the tarmac watching as soldiers ceremoniously carried the casket from the plane to the hearse. He remembered seeing Jackie's knees buckle as she started to sink to the ground, sobbing. Tom was able to catch her in time and support her before she hit the tarmac. They watched in silence as the hearse pulled away and drove out of sight.

From Dover, Tom flew back home to start planning the funeral. Jackie and Tom were told that the military would not release their son's body from Dover until they had chosen a funeral home and had a burial plot.

Jackie was to arrive in the morning, and for the next few days, their life consisted of looking at cemetery plots and talking to funeral directors, fielding questions from family, friends, and the press while trying to plan for the arrival of Joey's body and the funeral.

War is hell.

CHAPTER 16 "The Calls"
November 3rd, 2012

The cell phone started to ring as Billy was unlocking his front door. Six was at his side as he walked into the studio and placed the groceries on the kitchen counter while pulling his phone out of his back pocket. "Hello?" he answered, not recognizing the caller from the number displayed.

"Billy, it's Shannon."

Billy immediately recognized her voice and knew who she was. They had served together in CAPS, and Shannon had enlisted in the Army one year after he and Joey had gone in. They had remained in contact with each other over the years, and he considered her a good friend. "Hey, Shannon. It's good to hear from you. What's up?"

"Did you hear about Joey yet?" Shannon asked.

"What about Joey?" Billy questioned, feeling his chest starting to tighten.

"Billy…. I am so sorry, but Joey is dead. He died during an incoming barrage at the COP. I was one of the medics on the bird transporting the injured out. I recognized him right away. God, I hate this war!"

Billy let out this blood curdling scream as he slowly sank to his knees, dropping his phone as he fell to the floor. Shannon could hear Billy crying and muttering, "No… No… No… No. Not Joey. Not Joey."

Six came over and nuzzled Billy before laying down by his side and placing his head on Billy's lap.

Billy could hear Shannon calling out through the phone, "Billy, pick up the phone. Billy…. Billy, talk to me. Billy!

Shannon hears Joey mumble through the sobs, "It's not fair. It's just not fair. Not Joey. God, not Joey. I can't take this anymore. I wish I were dead. At least then this pain would stop."

Shannon tries once more to get Billy to pick up the phone. "Billy, pick up the phone. Talk to me. Billy, please…. talk to me." Then she hears the phone go dead.

Panicked, Shannon googles the emergency phone number to the local police department where Billy lives. She quickly dialed the number and told them what had just transpired in their phone conversation and that she was requesting a wellness check to be conducted. Shannon gave them Billy's phone number and the most recent address she had for him. Shannon also told them that Billy is a disabled veteran with a service dog and most likely has a weapon. As she hangs up the phone, she prays that they will make it to Billy in time. Shannon couldn't bear losing another one of her friends.

The Sheriff's Deputy pulls up in front of the studio where Billy and Six live. While sitting in his vehicle, Deputy Corbitt reviewed the information and waited for backup to arrive. A few moments later, Deputy Flynn pulls up and parks. Deputy Corbitt and Deputy Flynn both exit their vehicles to discuss the situation. Knowing that Billy is a veteran, they want to keep things calm. Upon reaching the front door, Deputy Corbitt knocks and calls out, "Mr. Rockwell?

"Yes, who is this?" Billy questions from inside.

"This is Deputy Corbitt and Deputy Flynn with the Sheriff's Office. We received a request to do a wellness check on you. Would you mind stepping outside so we can talk? Deputy Corbitt asks.

"Ummmmmmm, sure. I guess." Billy replies. Billy grabs Six and slowly opens the door.

"Mr. Rockwell, I am Deputy Corbitt, and this is Deputy Flynn. Do you mind stepping out onto the porch? We just need to ask you a few questions." As Billy and Six stepped out onto the front porch, Deputy Flynn asked, "Do you have a weapon on you that we need to know about?"

"No, not on me. I have one in my closet, though." Billy replied.

"I understand that you have gotten some bad news today." Deputy Flynn stated. "As a fellow veteran, I know how hard it can be to hear that one of your friends has died. I am sorry for your loss."

Billy closes his eyes to hold back the tears and quietly replies, "Thank you."

Deputy Flynn and Deputy Corbitt continue asking Billy questions and carefully weighing his answers. After a while, Deputy Flynn and Deputy Corbitt decide it is in the best interest of Billy to be taken to the VA for a psychiatric evaluation where he could be involuntarily detained for roughly up to 20 days for emergency diagnosis, evaluation, and treatment.

Upon arriving at the VA, Billy was escorted inside with Six, where he met with a caseworker named Judy Nazario. During the intake process, he was informed that his service dog would not be allowed to stay with him while in the VA and asked if he had anyone who could take care of Six during his stay. Billy informed Judy that his mom and dad had died in a car crash just a little over a month after he had graduated from basic. He was an only child and had just moved to the area, so he didn't know anyone well yet enough to ask them to watch Six for him. Judy sadly explained that since he had no one to watch Six while he was in the VA, Six would be taken to the county animal shelter. Judy went on to explain that he would have about three days to find someone to get his service dog out; otherwise, it would either be euthanized, based on his age and health, or Six would be put up for adoption.

Through tears, Billy choked out to the caseworker, "I can't lose Six. He's all I have… and I need him. I can't take another loss. I just can't!"

"I'm so sorry," Judy replied. "I hate this part of my job. Having to tell someone that they may lose their service dog is not something I ever thought I would have to do."

CHAPTER 17 "Six"
November 4, 2012 through November 15, 2012

The day weighed heavily on Judy's mind, thinking about Billy and how he might lose his service dog while he was a patient at the VA. Once she got home, she called her friend Annie. "Hi Annie, it's Judy."

"Yes, Judy, how are you doing? What's up?" Annie replied.

"Annie, do you still work at the county animal shelter?" Judy asked.

"Yes, I do. Why?" Annie responded.

"By any chance, do you know if a German Shepard was brought in today to the shelter?" Judy questioned.

"Yes, Judy, there was one. How did you know?" inquired Annie.

"Well, I normally don't get involved in this kind of thing, but we had a young veteran admitted today with a service dog. The dog's name is Six. Unfortunately, this veteran has no family or friends that can watch his service dog for him, and I don't think he will be getting out within the next three days. His parents are dead, and he just lost two friends who were still serving in the military. I really don't think he will survive another loss, so I was hoping that maybe you might know of someone who could take Six and watch him for a while until this veteran gets out of the VA." Judy replied.

"I am not sure," Annie responded, "I wish I could take him, but I can't. I already have two dogs, and my HOA doesn't allow more than two dogs per household. Also, the HOA has a limit on a dog's size, and Six exceeds that as well, so my friends in my neighborhood would not be able to take him either, but let me see what I can do."

"Thanks, Annie. I appreciate it. Just let me know one way or the other if you can find someone," replied Judy.

"Sure thing," Annie stated right before Annie and Judy said their goodbyes and ended the call.

After hanging up the phone, Annie hesitated but then dialed Tom's number. Unsure of how he would respond since she knew Tom didn't want anything to do with dogs, she was uneasy about what she was getting ready to ask him.

"Hey, Annie," Tom answered.

"Hi, Tom. I hope I caught you at a good time." Annie inquired.

"Sure, what's new?" replied Tom.

"Well….I am not sure where to begin… and I don't want to upset you, but I couldn't think of anyone else to ask who could possibly help." Annie stated hesitantly. "I just got off a call with Judy over at the VA. She has a young veteran who was just admitted. Since he doesn't have anyone who can watch his service dog for him while he is a patient, his dog was sent to the shelter. From what Judy said, it sounds like he will be a patient at the VA for longer than three days. As you know, that means his dog will be evaluated and either euthanized or put up for adoption, based on procedures of the shelter, if he can't find someone in the next few days to pet sit his dog for him. As far as I could tell, the dog is young and in good health, so this means adoption. You know how quickly a purebred that is highly trained will be adopted. So, considering what this veteran told Judy during intake, she is concerned that losing his service dog may push him over the edge. She stated that both his parents were dead, and he had recently lost a few friends who were still serving in the military. I know this is a lot to ask… but would you be willing to care for the dog while this veteran gets the medical attention he needs?"

There was an awkward silence before Tom spoke up. "Annie, I just don't know. While I want to help, I'm just not sure I can handle taking care of a dog. I mean, I could physically… but emotionally, you know how hard this will be for me. Are you sure that you don't have someone else who could take him?

"No, Tom, I don't," replied Annie. "I know this will be hard for you. I wouldn't ask you this favor if it were not for the fact that it is a veteran in need of help."

She heard Tom take a deep breath and slowly let it out as he muttered, "Ok… I will do it. What do I need to do?"

"Thank you, Tom," Annie said in a soft voice. "Just come to the shelter tomorrow anytime between 10:00am and 11:00am. I will be working and can get all the paperwork done before you arrive, and I will have the dog ready for you to pick up when you get to the shelter." With nothing more to be discussed, they said their goodbyes and hung up the phone.

Annie immediately dialed Judy to let her know that she had found a veteran by the name of Tom Johnson who would take care of the service dog. She gave Judy his address so that the veteran at the VA would know where to go to pick up his dog upon being released. As they ended their call, she asked Judy to get the required paperwork sent over to her before 10:00am the following day. "Make sure you get it signed by the owner of Six to allow the shelter to release the dog to Tom," Annie stated.

"Will do." Judy replied, "And thank you so much, Annie. You are a saint!"

The next day, Tom arrived at the shelter and went inside to meet up with Annie. "Hi, Tom. Thank you for doing this. Let me go get Six."

"Six?" Inquired Tom.

"Yes. Six is his name. He is a beautiful German Shepherd. I know you are apprehensive about watching him, but he is an amazing dog. I think once you get to know him, you might just come to enjoy his company." With that being said, Annie turned and went to the kennel area to retrieve Six.

Driving home, Tom noticed how alert and intuitive the dog seemed to be. It wasn't long before Six came over closer to Tom and laid down on the seat, resting his head on Tom's lap. Tom couldn't help but reach down to pet Six's head and think how warm and soft Six felt.

Upon parking in the driveway, Six quickly sat up and looked around. "Come on, boy," Tom said as he opened the door, got out, and waited for Six to exit the truck.

Just then, an eagle swooped down low and circled the truck. It then flew up, landed in a tree nearby, and looked down upon Tom and Six. Tom couldn't help but smile. It seemed that an eagle would show up at specific times now as a way to let him know that his son was watching from heaven and approving of his journey. He had talked with several other parents in the grief meetings he attended who had lost a child, and many had shared similar stories of hawks, dragonflies, dolphins, or other wildlife that seemed to appear at special moments that gave them comfort as the eagle did to Tom. Before his son's death, he would have scoffed at people who shared these accounts with him. But now, since he had experienced it, he was a believer. He knew his son was defiantly contacting him in various ways, and he didn't care if anyone thought he was crazy.

That night, Tom allowed Six to sleep with him on his bed. Tom wasn't sure about sharing his bed with Six, but he was willing to see how it would go. During the night, Tom started having a nightmare, and Six immediately moved closer to Tom and rested his head on Tom's chest. It woke Tom just enough to stop the nightmare but yet allowed him to drift back to sleep easily. This happened two more times during the night. The next morning, when Tom awoke, he realized that he had gotten the best night's sleep he had had in a long time.

Tom immediately got up and let Six out to do his business. While waiting for Six to get finished, he thought back about his night's sleep. Tom vaguely recalled being slightly wakened up by Six when he started having a nightmare and wondered if Six had been trained to do this. He would pay attention tonight to see if it happened again.

Six followed Tom everywhere he went, and Tom realized he was starting to enjoy Six's company. He also had to confess that the house didn't feel quite so empty with Six around. Over the next few nights, Six continued to help Tom with his sleep and, during the day, made a great companion and often had Tom laughing at his antics. So much so that he started thinking maybe he should look into getting a Service Dog, which really surprised him. After all, Tom never thought he would ever want a dog in his life again. But he had to admit, Six had been good for him.

CHAPTER 18 "Thanksgiving Day Wishes" November 15, 2012 through November 22, 2012

Billy had been doing well with the therapist and group sessions at the VA. He was missing Six and was glad when he was told that he was going to be released. He was given a ride back to his studio apartment so he could get his car and head off to pick up Six.

While on the drive, Billy thought about how strange it was that Tom's last name was Johnson. He knew it was a common last name, but the fact that his best friend Joey's last name was Johnson seemed like an odd coincidence. Just then, Joey spotted an eagle circling up ahead and watched as it flew down and landed on a fence post at the end of Tom's driveway. He felt Joey's presence, and in an odd way, it gave him comfort.

Billy stopped in front of the house and parked his car. Tom had been expecting Six's owner and heard the car coming up the drive, so he opened the door to let Six out. Billy watched as Six came running up to him, jumping all around and wiggling his body in sheer delight at being reunited. Tom laughed at the sight of Six so happy as he strolled up to Billy and extended his hand for a handshake.

"Hi, I'm Tom. I take it from the way Six is acting that you must be his owner."

Billy shook Tom's hand and replied, "Yes, I'm Billy. I want to thank you for taking care of Six for me. It is greatly appreciated. I don't know what I would have done if I had lost him. I hate to say it, but I would probably have become one of the 22-a-day who complete suicide. So thank you."

"I don't mean to pry, but what exactly happened?" Tom questioned.

"It's ok," Billy assured Tom. "I understand you're a veteran, so I don't mind talking about it with you. It seems like it has just been one loss after another. I was an only child. Then my parents were killed in a car crash not long after I graduated from basic, so I didn't have any family except for my military family." Billy paused as he kicked a clump of grass before continuing. "I had several friends I had served with in Civil Air Patrol and JROTC who also joined the military around the time I did. In fact, one of them had your last name. His first name was Joey." Billy stopped talking as he saw Tom's expression suddenly change.

"Did you serve in the Army?" Tom asked. "Were you out of Bragg? Was your friend Joey killed on October 19th?"

"Why yes," Billy answered. "How did you know?"

"Joey Johnson was my son." Tom choked out.

"Oh my God!" was all Billy could utter as he was so stunned. Both Tom and Billy teared up, and they immediately hugged each other. Just then, an eagle flew overhead and screeched, which broke the moment, giving them both a second to brush aside the tears from their eyes. After one more hug, they finally stepped apart, and Tom encouraged Billy to finish his story.

"Joey and I served together, but I was severely injured during our first deployment and was medically discharged. We had a friend named XinHua, who we knew from CAPS and JROTC. He was the only one of us who joined the Air Force. He texted me a note he wrote on August 17th saying that the stress had broken his will and that he hoped we would remember him fondly. He took his life, and I blamed myself for not seeing the signs. Then I got word from a friend that Joey had been killed, and it broke me. Thankfully, she called law enforcement to do a wellness check on me, or I probably would have taken my life, too."

"I am glad your friend made that call, and you are still here, Billy," Tom stated. "What I don't understand is why Six was taken to the pound. It's my understanding that he is your Service Dog, so why did they take him to the county shelter when they knew you were in the VA? I just don't get it. Do you know why?"

"My caseworker told me that the VA is not equipped to take care of a dog when someone gets admitted that requires an overnight stay or more. It doesn't matter if it is a service dog. It is happening with dogs that are pets, emotional support animals, and service dogs." Billy went on to say, "Since the patient cannot keep their dog with them in their hospital room... unless they have a family member or a friend who can watch their dog for them, the VA has no choice but to send these dogs to the shelter. Then, the shelters have rules they must follow so they don't get overrun. Most shelters consider these dogs brought in as an owner surrender. They will then evaluate the dog's age and overall health. They will usually only hold these dogs for up to three or four days to allow the owner time to return and get them or to find someone to pick them up and pet sit them for a while. Otherwise, these dogs are euthanized if they are deemed old and have health issues, or if they are younger and healthy, they are put up for adoption. Of course, most service dogs are purebreds, so people looking to adopt a dog come into the shelter and see a German Shepherd, Black Lab, Golden Retriever, or some other breed and will immediately be drawn to them. They will then get the dog out to play with it and start asking it to sit, lay down, stay, or some other command, and of course, the dog complies since it is highly trained. These people then walk out of the shelter with this dog, thinking they got lucky, not realizing they just adopted someone's Service Dog. Thankfully, you were able to watch Six for me, or I surely would have lost him. I'll tell you that would have totally destroyed me, and, to be honest, I am not sure what I would have done."

"That's just crazy!" Tom replied. "While I understand how heartbreaking losing a pet or emotional support dog could be, the loss of a Service Dog is devastating! Their training is usually $30,000.00 or more, and the service they have been trained to provide can be the difference between life or death for the handler. You would think that they would treat Service Dogs differently."

"Yeah, I know." Billy chimed in, "What's even crazier is that there are veterans who choose to forego getting necessary surgery, like a knee replacement, because they have no one to watch their service dog. Also, if they are willing to go into a drug or alcohol rehab or some mental health program to get better, they choose not to go because they can't risk losing their service dog. It's a shame that they are having to choose between getting the physical or mental health that they need and their service dog. You would think that someone would realize the problem and do something. Knowing what I know now, I wish there was something I could do about it, but my apartment complex doesn't allow pets. I can only have Six because he is a service dog."

"But wouldn't the dogs you take in be service dogs too?" Tom asked.

"While they would be service dogs, they would not be my service dog, so the rules of the ADA would not apply to them," Billy answered.

"I don't know about you, but I'm feeling a little parched. Want to come and join me for a glass of sweet tea? We can continue this conversation in the kitchen. I tend to do my best thinking there. Maybe we could figure this out. What do you say?" Tom asked.

"Sure," stated Billy. "I have nothing else I need to do. And hey, if we can come up with a solution, it will be well worth the time!"

With that, Tom, Billy, and Six returned to the house.

Over the next few days, Billy and Six continue coming over to Tom's to discuss how they could resolve the problem. Sometimes, Annie even joined them. One thing that they all keep coming back to is that Tom had the land and space to board dogs. That it really wouldn't take much to turn the barn into kennel space. That Annie had knowledge of kenneling dogs from working at the county shelter. And Billy would have the time to watch and care for the dogs. Tom also had the time, and he was softening to the thought of caring for a dog or two. He was even seriously considering getting a Service Dog for himself after experiencing how Six had helped him sleep.

On Thanksgiving Day, Annie, Billy, and Six came to Tom's house. Annie had brought a Waldorf salad and a pumpkin pie. Billy had brought a sweet potato casserole and the rolls. Tom had smoked a Turkey and grilled some green beans wrapped in bacon. The spread was amazing, and as they sat down at the table, Tom asked each one of them to share what they were thankful for.

Billy spoke up first. "I am thankful that you took in Six when I had no one to help me. I am thankful that I have gotten to know both you Tom, and you, Annie, on a much deeper level. I know it's been a very short time, but I feel like you are family already. I am also thankful that you included me in creating this Service Dog Program because it has given me a purpose, and I am truly feeling happy again. So, thank you. Thank you both."

Annie went next. "I am also thankful that you, Tom, you Billy, and, of course, Six, have come into my life. I am grateful that we were brought together, and I do have a feeling that Joey and God had something to do with it, and for that, I am so thankful. I, too, am thankful that I am a part of creating this place for service dogs. Because if I had a service dog and needed someone to watch him while I was in the hospital, I would want my service dog's place to be here on Tom's farm, being cared for by both of you."

"Oh my God, Annie! That's it!" Exclaimed Tom.

"What are you talking about?" Annie asked.
"The name," said Tom. "My Service Dog's Place. That is the perfect name for the program!"

Both Annie and Billy thought it was the perfect name, too. With the program's name decided, Annie could finish the paperwork to apply for a 501 (c) (3) status with the IRS.

Now, it was Tom's turn. "Well, I am thankful that we have now come up with the name for the program. I am also thankful to have you Annie, and you Billy, and, of course, Six in my life. And yes, Billy, I too feel like we are family. I call it *Bond Family'*." Tom went on to say, "Billy, I am thankful that we have met, and like Annie, I too feel Joey and God had something to do with it. I can't begin to tell you how healing it has been for me to get to know you. You have shared stories about Joey with me that I never knew about because I wasn't there when you were serving together in the Army. I know we have both cried at times, but we have laughed too. And it is comforting to know that someone else cared about him as much as I did and still do. But mostly, talking about Joey with you has brought me such joy and peace, and I am thankful for that."

Billy interrupted, "Tom, I am thankful for that too. I have to say that while I was in the VA, I thought about trying to find you, but I was too scared to try. I feared you would hate me because I survived, and Joey did not. And I have loved talking about Joey too. It's been very healing for me as well. While I would give anything to have Joey here with us, it amazes me that the tragedy of Joey being killed could have something good come out of it. And I promise you, Tom, Joey will never be forgotten as long as I have breath in me."

"Thank you, Billy," Tom replied. "You know, I never told anyone this, but my friend Bennie and I had made a pact that if one of us got killed while in Vietnam, the other was to find the family and let them know that they didn't die alone. And that they would always be remembered. But like you, Billy, I was too afraid to try to find Bennie's family after I returned."

CHAPTER 19 "My Service Dog's Place"
November 23, 2012 through December 24, 2012

Annie couldn't get Tom's regret out of her mind. She had observed so many positive changes in Tom recently. He had slowed way down on his drinking, and he enjoyed being around dogs, which were two things she never thought she would see happen. He seemed so much happier and calmer now, too. He deserved to have a happy life with no regrets hanging over his head. Would it be possible to track down Bennie's family? Could it be possible that some of his immediate family could still be alive? What a great gift to give Tom for Christmas, she thought, if she could just find them somehow. She knew Bennie's last name and where he was from due to Tom's stories, so she started an internet search with the information she had. Soon, she was able to find Bennie's obituary, which named his parents and siblings. It also gave the name of the town where they had held the funeral, so she surmised that this must be where Bennie's parents had been living at the time of his death. Annie continued to work on trying to find

Bennie's family and followed every lead she came across. In the meantime, she continued to help with My Service Dog's Place program by filling out and filing the papers with the IRS for it to become a 501 (c) (3). She also created a book of standard operating procedures and designed the different forms they would need to process the service dogs in and out of the program.

Tom and Billy had been making great progress on converting the barn into kennel space over the last few weeks. This morning, they were finishing up one of the last few kennels they were building in the barn when Billy suddenly stopped what he was doing and said, "Tom, I know this may sound crazy, but I feel Joey's presence with us today. I can't really explain it other than I can feel him. And I believe he had something to do with bringing us together and that he is so happy we are working on this program."

"I don't think it's crazy at all Billy". Tom replied. "I have been feeling him too. In fact, I truly believe he has come to me in several ways since he died. I also keep seeing this eagle at certain poignant times. Kind of like letting me know that I am on the right path, and I draw comfort from it."

"That just gave me the chills. I never told you this, but an eagle flew down and landed on the fence post right at the entrance to your driveway when I first came to meet you and pick up Six." Billy continued holding back the tears, "I also felt, at that moment, Joey was trying to let me know that things were going to be alright. God, I miss him."

As they started working again, Tom and Billy continued to talk. "I remember the day they came to notify me of his death," Tom uttered. "I had already experienced so many deaths during my time in Nam, but I was caught off guard by the death wail I heard coming out of my body as I sank to my knees upon receiving the news. Being able to talk with you and share stories about Joey and knowing that someone else loves him as much as I do and will remember him after I am gone gives me a lot of peace. I think that is one of my biggest fears. That Joey will be forgotten."

"Yeah, I know what you mean," Billy replied. "I remember Shannon calling me with the devastating news. I, too, recall this primal scream coming out of me. It shook me to my core. But I promise you, Tom, as long as I am alive, Joey will never be forgotten."

"Ya know, another thing I've realized is the importance of having a purpose. Something greater than self. I never would have thought about needing a purpose or finding a purpose to enrich my life and bring me joy and peace. I have truly been blessed that this purpose was bestowed upon me. It has been healing. Having you and Six in my life has been healing. And being able to talk with a fellow veteran, even though we have served at different times, has been healing." Tom cleared his throat before continuing, "I guess that is why when any of my veteran friends and I get together and talk, I always feel a little better."

"Funny you should say that, Tom," Billy replied. "I was reading an article a while back about how the Indians and other ancient cultures would require their warriors returning from battle to go to a sacred space with a shaman. They would have various time-honored traditions and rituals to help heal the spirit. They also would sit around the fire at night and talk. They would do this for months before being brought back into the fold of the tribe. Somehow, our society has forgotten how important this ritual is for those returning from a battlefield. If you think about it, due to technology and transportation today, we are in theater one day and home the next. Really doesn't give us much time to decompress and process our losses."

"Nope, it doesn't," Tom responded. "Probably the last soldiers who had any opportunity to have any time to discuss what they had been through and their losses were the ones who served in WWII. Most of them came home by ship, so they had a week or so together after leaving the battlefield before returning home. It makes me wonder if this is why the suicide rate is rising among our active duty and veteran population."

"Yes!" Billy answered. "I think so too! In fact, what I don't understand is why you are looked upon as being weak if you ask for help. You would think that the military would want not only physically healthy but mentally healthy soldiers. I know it was worse for those serving when you were in Tom, but it can still be a career breaker if you seek out help. They say it won't be, but I know it has been for several friends who are either still in or have gotten out. There is just such a stigma attached to it that so many just try to suck it up and stay quiet."

"It's crazy, for sure." Tom agreed. "You know, if our military would just make mental health a priority and require all soldiers returning from deployment to spend time with counselors, both individually and in group settings, for a specific amount of time after returning from a war zone, there would not be any stigma attached to anyone. Also, just like it is mandatory for everyone getting out to have a physical for physical injuries sustained in service to be noted, they need to make it mandatory for them to be assessed for mental injuries as well."

"You got that right. But the military doesn't like messy. They like a one size fits all. Let's face it; mental health is messy and definitely not a one size fits all." Billy chuckled. "And I definitely don't think those in power would ever consider it. They don't seem to care if we even have good working equipment when we are in a war zone. And let's not even talk about the rules of engagement. I think we are just a statistic and nothing more to them."

"Yep." Tom concurred. "You would think that they would realize that the only person who would not be affected by doing and seeing what has to be done in a war would be a psychopath. And let's face it, those who serve are not psychopaths."

"You're so right about that. You are so right! I do have to say, though, the one thing the military does right is to get us to understand that family isn't just by blood. It's who has your back. Like you said, Tom, it's *'bond family'*. And you and Annie are in my bond family for sure! Ok... now just one more screw, and I will have this kennel done. That leaves just one more kennel to build, and we will be finished with the inside!" Billy stated with pride as he stood and looked around the barn.

Tom responded, "Yes, sir, we are making great progress for sure! And like I said before, you're in my bond family too, Billy. Now.... I don't know about you, but I could use some lunch. What do you say we stop working for a bit and go get a bite to eat."

"Sounds good to me. I am famished." Replied Billy. "Let's go!"

CHAPTER 20 "Christmas Together"
December 25, 2012

Just like they did on Thanksgiving, Annie, Tom, and Billy had decided to spend Christmas day together. After all, they were family now. Each had placed their gifts to one another under the tree the night before in anticipation of this special day. They had decided to meet at Tom's for Christmas brunch and then open presents. Annie had brought an egg casserole, Billy had brought some fresh fruit, and Tom had made his famous homemade biscuits and gravy.

As they got seated around the kitchen table, Tom asked everyone to hold hands while they bowed their heads as he said a blessing.

After the blessing, Tom didn't miss a beat. "Sure smells good!" he said as he scooped a colossal helping of egg casserole onto his plate.

"You got that right!" Billy replied. "My mouth is watering!"

"I will have to concur." Annie agreed. "It does all look and smell delicious!"

After brunch, the three of them made their way into the living room near the Christmas tree and sat down. Six also came in and joined them, lying down on the rug in front of the fireplace.

Billy went straight to the tree, grabbed a big bone for Six, and gave it to him. Six immediately began wagging his tail and happily started to gnaw on it. Billy then turned, walked back to the tree, retrieved two matching wrapped boxes, and handed one to Tom and one to Annie. "It's not much," Billy stated as they started to unwrap his gift to them, "but I hope you like it."

Inside each box was a matching silver band bracelet with the words **BOND FAMILY** engraved on the outside and on the inside *JOEY JOHNSON 2/1/89 - 10/19/12 NEVER FORGOTTEN!*

Tom got misty-eyed upon reading the inscription. Tom spoke softly as he placed it on his wrist, "Thank you, Billy. This is a perfect gift, and to me it is priceless."

"Yes!" Exclaimed Annie. "It is beautiful! Thank you! I will wear it with pride."

"I am so glad you like it. I got one for me too." Billy replied as he rolled up his sleeve to show off his bracelet. "I know we haven't known each other for very long, but it feels like I have known you both forever. I love you both dearly. Thank you for bringing me into your life."

"Love you too, Billy!" Annie said as she gave him a hug.

"You are family," Tom stated as he choked back the tears. "You always will be!"

"My turn!" Said Annie as she made her way to the tree. First, she handed Billy a medium size box that had an envelope inside.

Billy opened the envelope and started to read out loud what was printed on the piece of paper that had been tucked inside. "You are now the proud owner of a St. Croix Legend Xtreme Spinning Rod. It has integrated poly curve, advanced reinforcing technology, taper enhancement technology, super high-modulus SCVI graphite with FRS in the lower section for maximum power and strength with reduced weight, as well as high-modulus/high-strain SCV graphite with FRS and carbon-matte scrim for unparalleled strength, durability, and sensitivity. Hopefully, this will remedy the stories of how the big one got away! Love always, Annie."

"Your fishing pole is in the closet in the hall," Annie said when Billy finished reading. "I wanted you to be surprised, and it's kind of hard to wrap a fishing pole up without people figuring out what it is. I know how much you enjoy fishing with Tom, and you deserve a nice rod like his to use when you guys go down to your favorite fishing hole."

"Holy Catfish!" Billy gasped in awe at this expensive and thoughtful gift. He jumped out of his chair, gave Annie a quick bear hug, and then ran to the hall closet to retrieve the rod as he shouted, "Annie…. Thank you. Thank you. Thank you! I can't believe it… this is so awesome!"

Then Annie handed Tom a little bit smaller box. Tom, too, had an envelope inside his box. Like Billy, he opened the envelope, took out the piece of paper, and began to read it aloud. "My dearest Tom, You should never have to live with regrets. I am pleased to inform you that I found Bennie's family. His mother, Deborah, and sister, Ashley, are still alive and doing well." Tom looked up from the paper at Annie in a state of shock. With tears rolling down his cheeks, he asked, "How did you find them? I can't believe this! Annie, are you sure it is Bennie's family?"

Annie sat down beside Tom and wrapped her arms around him. "Yes, Tom. They are Bennie's family. Now go on and finish reading the letter."

"They live in a small town about 5 hours away and are very excited to meet you." Tom choked out, trying to hold back the tears. "I have already arranged for us to visit them on December 27th. I have secured a hotel suite at the Marriott so we can enjoy our time together and not be rushed getting back home. Merry Christmas! Love always, Annie."

Embracing Annie in a big hug, Tom proclaimed, "This is the best present I could ever get! Oh my God,

Annie!!! You are so good to me. I love you so much! Thank you… thank you!"

"You are most welcome, my knight in shining armor." Annie playfully replied. "I love you too!"

Now it was Tom's turn to pass out the presents. First, Tom grabbed a very small box and handed it to Billy, saying. "As the saying goes, big things can come in small packages."

Billy tore off the wrapping paper and opened the box. Inside was a key. "Is this a key to your house?" Billy asked.

"No," said Tom. "Even better. It is a key to your new home! I have purchased a double-wide modular home and titled it in your name. It is to be installed on the farm down by the barn. It is yours, so you need to give your landlord a 30-day notice that you will be vacating your studio apartment because you are now a homeowner. The home should be completely installed, hooked up to all utilities, and be ready for you to move in within the next 2 to 3 weeks. After all, you are family, and I want you to live on the farm, too, because one day it will become yours."

Billy was dumbfounded. "What? Are you kidding me?" Billy croaked out between sobs. He stood up and ran over to Tom and threw his arms around him. "Oh my word, I don't know what to say. Tom, are you sure?"

"Billy, I have never been more sure of something in my life. Well… I take that back. There is one thing that I am more convinced of, and that leads me to Annie." Tom once again walked over to the tree, grabbed the last small box, made his way back over to Annie, and handed it to her.

Annie started to unwrap the box and jokingly questioned. "Tom, did you get me a key to your tractor?" It was a good guess since Tom was always saying he was going to teach her how to drive it, but he assured her it wasn't. Annie continued to open the box, not noticing that Tom had dropped down in front of her on one knee. As Annie opened the box, she saw the most beautiful diamond ring inside and gasped.

Tom removed the ring from the box and looked lovingly up at Annie, and said, "Annie, will you marry me?"

Now, it was Annie who was crying. "Oh my God, Tom. Yes, YES! I will marry you!" She replied as she let Tom slip the ring onto her finger while she began to smother him in kisses.

"All I have to say," interjected Billy, "is this is one Christmas I will never forget!"

CHAPTER 21 "New Beginnings"
December 26, 2012 through December 30, 2012

Tom and Annie spent the day after Christmas getting packed and ready for their trip to visit Bennie's family. Tom went into town to have a couple of pictures he had cherished of Bennie and himself during the time they had served together made into a collage. He also purchased two nice frames to put them into. Tom hoped that Bennie's mom and sister would like seeing these pictures as much as he had enjoyed seeing the pictures of Joey that Billy had shared with him not too long ago. He also bought some lovely wrapping paper and some ribbon. He would have Annie wrapped them up because she was so much better at it than he was. She just had this knack of making a present look so pretty that you kind of hated to rip it open.

Tom and Annie got up early and said their goodbyes to Billy as they finished their coffee before hitting the road for the 5-hour trip. Billy assured them that he and Six would take good care of the place while they were gone and not to worry about a thing.

Tom and Annie discussed so many different topics on the drive that the time rushed by. They found the hotel, got checked in, and settled before starting their drive to Bennie's mom's house, where they were all to meet for dinner.

"I'm not going to lie, Annie," Tom stated as they started to pull into the driveway, "I'm really nervous."

"That's understandable," replied Annie. "But remember how excited you were when you met Billy, and he shared all those wonderful stories with you about Joey? I am sure Deborah and Ashley will be just as excited to hear stories about Bennie that only you can share with them. And I am sure they will have questions that only you can answer. Answers that will give them comfort. And comfort in knowing someone else loved

Bennie the way they do and that Bennie will never be forgotten."

Just then, Tom spotted an eagle soaring in the sky ahead of them and pointed. "Look, Annie," Tom exclaimed. "It's an eagle!" Tom and Annie watched in wonder as the eagle glided through the air so effortlessly and then swooped down so gracefully to land in a tree near the house. Tom parked the truck, turned to Annie, and said, "Annie, that's a sign from Joey that everything will be ok. Let's go meet Deborah and Ashley." With that, Tom hopped out of the truck and grabbed the gifts. He then walked around the truck and opened Annie's door for her to get out.

"Always my knight in shining armor," Annie stated as she smiled and took Tom's hand. Then together, they walked up the sidewalk. Before they could even make it to the front door, both Deborah and Ashley came rushing out to greet them.

"You must be Annie," Ashley said as she gave Annie a hug. "It's so nice to meet you!"

"And you must be Tom," Deborah stated as she embraced him into her arms. "Come, both of you. Supper is ready. Let's sit and enjoy our meal together. Ashley, go grab a bottle of wine and pour us all a glass."

The house was cozy, and the dining table was filled with bowls of different vegetables and trays of meats. "I forgot to ask what you like to eat." Deborah said, "So, I made several different dishes."

"What a spread!" Tom replied. "If it tastes just half as good as it looks, I will gain at least five pounds before the night is over."

Soon, everyone was chatting like they had known each other forever. It felt comfortable, like being with familiar friends and family. Mainly, the conversation consisted of sharing stories of Bennie from his early years and those of his time in service.

After dinner, Tom presented Deborah and Ashley with his gifts. They were so grateful that Tom had shared with them pictures they had never seen before of Bennie. Through laughter and tears, they continued to share stories. Suddenly, Deborah said in a hushed and solemn tone, "Tom, we were told that Bennie had lingered on for days after being injured but that the medics couldn't get to him and the others who were injured. I hate knowing he suffered for so many days before he died."

"Who told you that Deborah?" Tom inquired.

"I don't remember who exactly told us that," Deborah answered. "But I do remember them saying he wouldn't have survived his injuries even if they had been able to treat him right away."

"Well, whoever told you that was wrong," Tom replied. "I was there when we got attacked. And Bennie died almost instantly." Tom stopped momentarily to clear his throat and wipe away the tears that were starting to fall before continuing. "Although he was still breathing when I got to him, he was unresponsive. In fact, I was holding him in my arms when he passed. It happened so fast I truly don't think he felt a thing."

"Oh, Tom, thank you for letting me know that. I have struggled all these years with the thought that he was in excruciating pain for days before he died in the jungle." Deborah replied softly. "I had also been haunted by the notion that he died alone."

"No, ma'am," Tom said as he closed his eyes and reflected on that time in Nam. "Bennie was not alone when he died. He was my best friend. I loved him. I still do. He was my brother and always will be. There is not a day that goes by that I don't think of him, and as long as there is breath inside of me, Bennie will never be forgotten."

"Tom, I am so grateful for you sharing this information with us," Ashley responded. "I can see that you genuinely loved Bennie. And it is so comforting to know he didn't die alone. That he had someone who loved him by his side when he passed. I can never begin to thank you enough for this information. It gives us peace."

"You are welcome," Tom replied. "I am just so sorry it took this long to come and meet with you. You know, Bennie and I had made a promise to each other that if one of us died, the other would go meet with the family. It has weighed heavily on me all these years, that I never kept that promise. And had it not been for Annie finding you, I don't know that I ever would have. Not because I didn't want to, but because I was too afraid you would hate me for not being able to save Bennie." Tom paused as he composed himself. "It's funny how you can allow those false beliefs you have in your head hold you back. All I can say is Bennie was right. He said he had an awesome family and that I would love meeting you. I am just sorry I let my fear get in the way of doing it sooner."

"Hey, Tom," Annie interjected. "I hate to break the mood, but it's almost midnight. Maybe we should say our goodbyes and get back to the hotel so that we all can get some sleep."

"Wow!" stated Ashley. "Where has the time gone? It doesn't feel like we have been talking that long, but the clock doesn't lie."

Deborah chimed in, "It is way past my bedtime for sure, but I am so glad you came. Come give me a hug goodbye and promise me that you will keep in touch with us."

Tom and Annie gave both Deborah and Ashley some heartfelt hugs, assuring them that they would be keeping in touch. Tom also invited them both to his New Year's Eve get-to-gather as they left.

The next day, Tom and Annie drove to the cemetery where Bennie had been laid to rest. They found his gravesite with ease using the directions that Deborah and Ashley had provided to them the night before. Tom knelt down by the grave and wiped away some dried grass that had gotten stuck on the headstone.

Tom reached into his pocket and pulled out a penny, a nickel, a dime, and a quarter and placed it on top of the headstone as he told Bennie that he missed him and would never be forgotten.

Walking back to the car, Annie asked Tom why he had placed the coins on Bennie's headstone.

Tom replied, "Well, it's kind of a tradition that started during the Vietnam War. It is supposed to be a way to let the deceased soldier's family know that somebody stopped by to pay their respects. If you leave a penny, it means you visited. A nickel means you and the deceased soldier trained at boot camp together. If you served with the soldier, you leave a dime. A quarter is very significant because it means that you were there when that soldier was killed."

"Oh," Annie replied. "What a nice tradition."

CHAPTER 22 "It's in the Stars"
December 31, 2012

Tom and Annie are finishing the final tasks that need to be completed before the guests arrive for the New Year's Eve party when Tom says to Annie, "Hard to believe that I met you just a year ago today."

"I know," Annie said as she kissed Tom on the cheek. "Seems like we have known each other forever."

"I am so lucky you came into my life," Tom responded. "You have definitely changed my life for the better."

"And you've made a positive impact in mine," Annie replied.

Just then, the doorbell rang as the first guest arrived. Tom answered the door and immediately greeted Anthony with a hug and asked if he could continue to welcome the other guests as they arrived so he could get the steaks going on the grille.

"You got it, Tom!" Anthony replied. "My pleasure." It wasn't long before the party was in full swing, and once again, the house and backyard was alive with the laughter and chatter of family and friends.

"Ok, everyone!" Tom shouted. "Steaks are done, so everyone come inside and let's eat!"

After dinner, everyone made their way out into the backyard to continue enjoying each other's company. While some challenged each other to a game of corn-hole, ping-pong, or 8-ball, others found comfortable chairs and were chatting, catching up with each other's lives.

"Tom, I hear that you and Annie got engaged at Christmas. Is that right?" Mitch asked.

"Yep. It's true." Tom replied. "A lot has happened in this last year. A lot of great things. Annie being one of them."

"Well, you know Tom…. if you ever want to tie the knot, I am now a minister. I have already performed a few weddings since I was ordained. You know, I must say, it gives me a good feeling to be a part of an important milestone in someone's life. Especially if it is someone you know and care about."

"I bet it does!" Tom answered. "I do have one question, though, if someone wanted to get married right away but didn't have the paperwork done. Would you still be able to marry them?"

"I could, but it technically wouldn't be legal until the marriage license was signed. Why, what are you thinking?" Asked Mitch.

"Not sure yet." replied Tom. "But let me get back to you on that." Tom then turned and made his way over to Annie.

"Hi, sweetie!" Annie greeted Tom, followed by a quick kiss. "What's up?"

"Annie, how would you feel if we got married tonight," Tom asked. "Right here in front of our family and closest friends. In front of our *Bond Family*. I know this is sudden, but it just feels right. I can't think of a more appropriate place for us to say our *I do's*. Can you?"

Annie looked at Tom and inquired, "Are you sure? I mean, I know I love you, Tom, or I wouldn't have said yes when you asked me to marry you. But are you sure? Are you sure this is really what you want to do?"

Tom replied, "Annie, I have never been more sure about something in my whole life." Just then, an eagle flew into view and circled over the couple. "Look, Annie. Another sign from Joey. I think he is giving us his blessing." The eagle made one final majestic circle before disappearing into the woods.

"But where will we find a minister on this short notice? Annie questioned. "And what about the marriage license? While I think being married right here and now is a great idea, I don't see how it would be possible."

"I just found out Mitch is now an ordained minister. He could marry us. He did say it wouldn't be legal as far as the government is concerned until we got the marriage certificate signed, but he said we could get that done on Wednesday since the courthouse will be closed tomorrow. What do you say?" Tom asked.

"Then I say Yes!" Annie exclaimed as she leaned in and gave Tom a long, passionate kiss. When they finally pulled apart from their embrace, Tom left Annie and made his way back over to Mitch.

Upon locating him, Tom asked, "Hey Mitch, what do you say about performing an impromptu wedding for Annie and me? We know it won't be officially legal until we can get the paperwork done on Wednesday, but would you do me the honor of officiating our nuptials?"

"Really? Right here and right now?" Mitch questioned.

"Yep. Really. Right here and right now." Replied Tom.

"Hey, everybody! Can I have your attention, please! Can I have your attention please!!!!" Shouted Mitch. Once Mitch saw he had everyone's attention, he continued, "I am so excited to announce that we have been invited to Tom and Annie's wedding!"

"When's it going to be?" Mitch heard Anthony ask.

"It's going to be right here and right now!" Mitch answered. "Billy and a few of you guys, please grab some chairs and place them so there is an aisle-way between a few chairs on the left and a few on the right leading up to the fire pit. And, Tom and Annie, please make your way to me. As the chairs were being set up, Tom, Annie, and Mitch whispered plans over in the corner.

"Ok… everyone, please find a seat, and Tom, you, Billy, and Martha come with me up to the fire pit." Stated Mitch. "And Annie, make your way to the back of the chairs." Annie was handed a beautiful red poinciana that someone had plucked off a plant nearby in a planter as she made her way to where she had been directed to go.

The sun had just about set as Mitch asked if anyone in the crowd could come up with a suitable song to play from their phone connecting to the speakers via Bluetooth.

"Too easy" replied JR. "I got this!"

The sun had just faded into night, and the strings of solar light bulbs popped on as Mitch positioned Martha on his right and Tom and Billy on his left. Just then, JR started the music. It looked magical as Annie slowly walked down the aisle to Tom to the song 'Can You Feel The Love Tonight' by Elton John. Once Annie reached the point where she was to stand in front of Mitch, JR faded the music out.

"To everyone gathered here today, it is my honor and privilege to join together Tom and Annie in holy matrimony," Mitch stated. "Tom, do you promise to cherish Annie always, to honor and support her in sickness and in health, and to be true to her until death do you part?"

"I do," replied Tom.

Then Mitch turned to Annie and asked, "And Annie, do you promise to cherish Tom always, to honor and support him in sickness and in health, and to be true to him until death do you part?"

"I do," answered Annie.

"By the power vested in me by American Marriage Ministries and the state of Tennessee, I now pronounce you husband and wife. Tom, you may now kiss your bride."

Like a rehearsed script, the fireworks started exploding in the distance just as Tom leaned in to kiss Annie.

Then Mitch announced, "Everyone, let me be the first to introduce you to Mr. & Mrs. Johnson."

Epilogue

Anyone who has been on a battlefield will tell you that if they close their eyes and think, they can be right back there. They can still hear the gunfire and grenades. They can smell the gun powder and taste the dust in the air. They can still see it all in vivid color. The yelling, the rushing, the shooting, the blood... the chaos... the confusion... they can be brought right back there... all by simply closing their eyes.

They will find themselves asking, at times... Why did I get to live while those who I served with and loved had to die? Why did I get to live without sustaining any physical injuries while those who I served with and loved got injured? Why me and not them?

Whether you have served in the military or not, we have all experienced life, both good and bad. We don't always get the miracle we want or that we think we deserve. Sometimes we get the healing, we get the rescue, we get the safety. Other times, we get the pain, the suffering, the loss. But, in both cases, you can find peace.

As a mother of a son, who was killed in Afghanistan, I have learned that the secret comes down to the choices we make. But the trick is to understand what choices we really have. While we may want to change someone else's behavior, this is something we do not have the power to do. While we may want to change the events of what happened in the past, that is not realistic. It can't be done. We do, however, have control of ourselves. It is the only thing we truly have control of… how we choose to handle ourselves physically, mentally, emotionally, and spiritually in the moment and in the future. While the past is always present in our lives, how we choose to come to remember and view the events of the past is subject to change as we change.

It is learning to cast off what we may have been taught to believe that is unhealthy for us and relearning a healthy belief system.

How many times in your life have you been told, or you have thought, that it is not ok to be angry, or sad, or fearful, or guilty, or grateful, or happy, or lonely, or inadequate, or successful, or strong, or empty, or helpless, or resentful, or satisfied, or proud, or jealous, or a failure? How many times have you beat yourself up because you felt those emotions?

Having emotions is perfectly healthy. There is nothing wrong with you. Something has happened to you, so you're supposed to have these feelings. Sometimes it's supposed to hurt. Sometimes you are supposed to be angry or sad, or guilty or fearful. Learning to embrace and sit with your emotions is hard to do, but it can be healing. Recognize that these are common human reactions to events in life, and it is ok to have these feelings.

Take responsibility (this is a choice) for your own actions, thoughts, and feelings. It's up to you how you decide to view events or situations, past, present, and future. Will you view them as an obstacle or an opportunity? After all, actions, thoughts, and feelings are powerful. They can be used for both good or bad. You can learn to harness that power to change your emotional state. To improve and even transform your situation for the better if you so choose.

I am not saying this is easy to do. We have had a lifetime of creating bad habits, false narratives, and negative beliefs about our life and ourselves, even ones that are not true, but they are still torture. It is always easier to try and lay the blame on someone else than to take responsibility for our part in any situation. But don't give your power away. Although it will take work on your part to change how you embrace the past, the now, and the future, it is work worth doing.

There is no magic wand that can make everything all better. There are no shortcuts, and there is not a one size fits all solution. Also, realize that no matter how hard you work to be the best you that you can be, overcoming negative feelings, false narratives, and bad habits is not a once and for all attainment. They come back. There are many tools out there to help you crawl, walk, or sit with your trauma. Know it, speak to it, paint it, draw it, build it. Just stay with it. And remember that this is a lifelong journey, so be kind to yourself.

For those who want to start their journey, there are a lot of great books, programs, and organizations out there to assist you in and on your way.

I have listed a few great books on the following pages, and I know that what you choose to do with that list is up to you.

My Warrior's Place is currently creating a database called Operation Tango Yankee that will provide a FREE platform for non-profit organizations to promote themselves and allow those in need to find them.

If you know of a non-profit that should be in this database, please have them go to www.otyusa.org and enter in their information.

Additionally, for a small donation to support My Warrior's Place and its programs, any business that supports our American Heroes and their families can be listed in this database as well. To get your business listed request that we contact you through our "contact us" page on our website at https://www.mywarriorsplace.org/

My Warrior's Place Programs: My Service Dog's Place, Operation Solid 7, FAVE Boating Expeditions, Everyday Heroes USA and our MWP Retreat Center.

RECOMMENDED BOOKS
(in no particular order)

While there are many great self-help books out there, these are just a few books that I have read, and recommend to others. I hope you enjoy them and are inspired by them as much as I was.

- Kelly Kowall

The Body Keeps the Score by Bessel van Der Kolk

The Four Agreements by Don Miguel Ruiz

The Fifth Agreement by Don Miguel Ruiz

Mastery of Self by by Don Miguel Ruiz Jr.

Inner Bonding by Margaret Paul

Healing Grief by James Van Praagh

The Dark Side of the Light Chasers by Debbie Ford

Relationships by Drs. Les & Leslie Parrott

Life Strategies by Phillip C. McGraw, Ph.D.

Peace Under All Circumstances by Matthew Brownstein

Good Grief by Deborah Morris Coryell

The Power of Now by Eckhart Tolle

Embracing Your Inner Critic by Hal Stone & Sidra Stone

Man's Search for Meaning by Victor E Frankl

The Power of Self-Esteem by Nathaniel Branden, PH.D.

Be Full of Yourself by Patricia Lynn Reilly

Why Are the Casseroles Always Tuna? by Darcie D. Sims

Awakening the Mind, Lightening the Heart by The Dalai Lama

ABOUT MY WARRIOR'S PLACE AND ITS PROGRAMS

My Service Dog's Place is an actual program of the nonprofit My Warrior's Place. It was created because Kelly had been contacted by the VA at different times on behalf of a few veterans who had been admitted into the VA, and their Service Dog had been taken to the county animal shelter. These veterans knew Kelly and asked for her help. Each time she was contacted, Kelly retrieved their service dog and took care of it until the veteran was released from the VA and could be reunited with their service dog.

During COVID, a veteran in his early 30's came to My Warrior's Place with his service dog to stay at the retreat center so that he could be near the VA where he was to have a heart valve transplant, prior to being admitted. This veteran was going to call off his surgery because he had no one to watch his service dog while he was going to be in the VA. Kelly talked to the veteran and even asked, "Don't you understand that you will die if you don't get this transplant surgery?" And his reply was, "Yes, but I will die if I get out of the VA and don't have my Service Dog."

This was the turning point in which Kelly and the board members of My Warrior's Place decided that something had to be done, so they created the My Service Dog's Place program with the help of many volunteers.

My Warrior's Place provides support for our American Heroes (Military, Law Enforcement or Firefighters - those currently serving and those who have served) and their immediate family members, as well as, the Families of the Fallen.

Other programs that My Warrior's Place offers are:

Operation Solid 7 – This program provides retreats and workshops using time-honored wisdom, education, holistic approaches, and techniques to bring about healing and hope. It also provides education and information to help lower the suicide rate of our American Heroes.

FAVE Boating Expeditions – Provides memorable fishing and pleasure boat excursions, as well as, kayak and canoe trips.

Everyday Heroes USA – This program helps to provide relief for catastrophic and tragic events.

The MWP Retreat Center – Provides cottages and RV Pads for respite and vacations in a healing environment.

To make a donation to help support the American Heroes we honor, or for more information about My Warrior's Place, go to www.mywarriorsplace.org.

Made in the USA
Columbia, SC
13 September 2023

22813634R00111